Life Planning:

Learning to Make Every Day Count!

John C. Enelamah

Dedication

I dedicate this book to Professor Vincent Anigbogu who recently turned 70 years old, and his dear wife, Mrs. Peggy Anigbogu. Prof and Mama Peggy, as we fondly call them, together bear a tremendous burden for the African continent. Tirelessly investing in and paving the way for future generations of Africans, especially those yet unborn.

CONTENTS

ACKNOWLEDGMENTS

All good work is a team effort. In writing this book, I worked with some special people who put in extraordinary and painstaking effort, despite the constraints of time. I am grateful to all of you.

I would also like to acknowledge the special individuals whose lives and work provided the context for this book and made the writing both necessary and compelling. This includes Richard Winwood, Hyrum Smith, Alan Lakein, Abraham Maslow, Richard L. Kramer, Peter J. Daniels, Alfred Nobel, Warren Buffet, and especially Sunday Adelaja and Benjamin Franklin. Some of you now belong to the ages, but you have all left your footprints on the sands of time. I thank my extended family, especially my mother, Mrs. Elizabeth Enelamah, the matriarch of the family, for all their support. I would like to thank my dearest wife, Dr. Ngozi Eñelamah, and our three children, Isaac-John, Sean-David, and Joanna-Pearl. You make life worth living. Finally, I thank God for the inspiration to write and to keep writing.

INTRODUCTION

Overview of Laws of the Universe

This book is about life planning and presupposes that life on Earth is governed by fixed laws. In my book *Understanding the Laws of the Universe: Enduring Principles for Building and Maximizing Life on Earth,* I share some of these laws which make life on Earth predictable. In this book, *Life Planning: Learning to Make Every Day Count*, though the laws are mutually reinforcing, I primarily focus on the application of the laws of goals, time, planning, and purpose.

In this introduction, we are taking a look at the overview of the Laws of the Universe. This is to give us an insight into the fundamental principles that govern both the Universe and our individual journeys through life. These Laws of the Universe are not just theoretical concepts; they are practical tools for achieving success, fulfillment, and significance in our lives. We will define key concepts such as the Law of Thought, the Law of Planning, the Law of Goals, and the Law of Time, setting the stage for effective life planning. But first of all, what is the Universe?

What is the Universe?

The Universe is everything including time, space, matter, and all the energy that space contains. It includes us, the Earth, the Moon, the Sun, the planetary systems, and all the millions of galaxies. The Earth's galaxy is the Milky Way. The

Sun is part of hundreds of billions of stars that make up the Milky Way and most of these stars have their own planets known as exoplanets. The Milky Way is only one of billions of galaxies. All the stars in all the galaxies and everything else that cannot be observed are part of the Universe.

How Big is our Universe?

Have you ever given thought to or considered how big the universe is? The universe is about 93 billion light-years in diameter, and one light-year is equivalent to 9 trillion kilometers. That is how big the universe is. This is just the observable universe; the one that is not observable may as well be hundreds larger than the one that is observable. How was the universe formed? This may answer the question of the size of the universe. According to the Holy Bible, God spoke the universe into existence.

Hebrews 11:3
3 Through faith, we understand that the worlds (the Universe) were framed by the word of God, so that things which are seen were not made of things which do appear.

God created the universe by His spoken Word, and the Universe is still expanding. There is no clear scientific explanation for the expansion of the Universe, but there is a Biblical explanation. The word God spoke to form, command, and frame the universe has never been recalled by Him. Therefore, potentially, the Universe is still expanding at the rate at which it was first created when the word of God was first spoken, which is possibly a speed that even exceeds the speed of light. What is the immediate implication of this? It simply means there is no end to the universe. The study of the Universe is part of science. Science is an important subject of study, and scientists are God's gift to humanity. Scientists are important because they discover laws.

What is a Scientific Law?

A scientific law or laws of science are statements based on repeated experiments or observations that describe or predict a range of natural phenomena. Scientific laws are not suggestions. Are there laws that govern success on earth? In summary, yes. In creating the earth, God employed certain laws and subjected the earth to these laws. Nations and individuals that discover and apply these laws will naturally rise to the top irrespective of their religious persuasion. These laws are called the laws of the Universe.

The Laws of the Universe

1. **The Law of Thought**: Thoughts are things! God's works are the product of His thoughts, and His works are great because His thoughts are deep (Psalm 92: 5). In this life, you cannot rise above your thoughts, and God cannot change you until He changes the way you think (Romans 12:2 NLT). Your thoughts form your mindset, and your mindset shapes your destiny. We are to carefully guard our hearts as the contents determine the course or boundary of our lives (Proverbs 4:23).

2. **The Law of Goals:** Goals are dreams with a deadline. Goals give direction to our lives and make decision-making easier. Unless we set clear SMART goals, we are likely to go round in circles, running from pillar to post with a measure of confusion and with no clear sense of direction. What is a SMART goal? SMART goals are specific, measurable, achievable, realistic, and time-bound. When we have no goals, our problems become our goals.

3. **The Law of Words:** What are words? Words are spiritual containers that contain life or death. We have to be careful about words. Death and life are in the power of the tongue (Proverbs 18: 21). If you want to live a long and prosperous life, you have to choose your words carefully.

4. **The Law of Time:** Time is everything. It is both a limited and limiting resource. The first thing God created in starting the work of creation is time (Genesis 1: 1). God created time to dimension life on earth. Therefore, time is life. What you do with your time is what you have done with your life.

5. **The Law of Purpose:** What is purpose? According to the dictionary, purpose is the reason something is created or done or the reason something exists. The law of purpose states that all things are created on purpose and for a purpose. At the beginning of creation, the earth was without form, void, and darkness was on the face of the deep (Genesis 1:2). God solved the problem of formlessness by bringing purpose. He brought content

and creation to fill the void and commanded light to replace darkness. Unless the purpose of a thing is known and understood, abusive or inadequate use is unavoidable.

6. **The Law of Vision or Visualization:** Many are the eyes that look, but few are the eyes that see. What is vision? It is both the ability to see and to see beyond the ordinary. Stephen Covey wrote that all things are created twice; first is the mental creation and then the physical creation. Unless you see it, you cannot have it. God has a divine vision for every individual on Earth. Paul said, "Therefore, King Agrippa, I was not disobedient to the heavenly vision" (Acts 26:18 NKJV)."

7. **The Law of Faith:** What is faith? Faith believes in the impossible, hears the inaudible, and sees the invisible. Faith understands that with God all things are possible, and that all things are possible to him who believes (Matthew 19: 26; Mark 9:23). You are therefore your own limitation. We are to stretch our faith for God is an elastic God.

8. **The Law of Prayer:** Prayer is not only a potent force but the most powerful force on earth. What is the law of prayer? According to a paraphrase of Philippians 4:6, the law of prayer simply states that "we are not to worry about anything, but we should pray about everything, and remember to thank God when we pray and to keep praying until the answer comes." Jesus said, "And all things whatsoever you shall ask in prayer, believing you shall receive (Matthew 21:22)."

9. **The Law of Action:** Nothing happens until we make it happen. Every day we are to get up and go, trusting God along the way. We are to have an action orientation to life. God gets things done. According to Proverbs 20: 4, "The sluggard will not plow by reason of the cold; therefore, shall he beg in harvest, and have nothing." We must be diligent and learn to act promptly.

10. **The Law of Systems:** What is a system? In a system, the most talented person can walk away, but the system will continue. Unless something is systematic, it cannot be sustainable. Our human body is made up of thirteen organ systems. The developed world is made up of a concentric circle of systems, including an economic system, a communication system, an education system, a waste disposal system, a health system, etc. In creating the earth, God established systems that ensured He would not need to return to activate the earth. Each day gives birth to night, and each night gives birth to day. According to Genesis 8: 22, while the earth remains, seedtime and harvest, cold and heat, summer and winter, and day and night shall not cease. Why will seedtime and harvest, cold and heat, summer and winter, and day and night not cease? This is because they are systems within a universal system. They are part of the laws of the universe.

11. **The Law of Conversion:** The law of conversion is about how we use our time. Unless time is converted into products, goods, and services, we might not be able to account for time, which is our life. The recipe for poverty

and penury is failing to convert your time into products, goods, and services. What you have done with your time is what you have done with your life. Therefore, life management is time management.

12. **The Law of Decisions:** Nothing becomes dynamic until it becomes specific. We must be decidedly decided. The main reason we vacillate and procrastinate is because of fear, especially fear of the consequences of our actions. However, when we procrastinate, we only delay the inevitable. We have to face our future daily. There is nothing to fear in life except fear itself. A lack of decision is a decision in itself.

13. **The Law of Persistence:** We are called to persevere and endure. We must continue to keep keeping on. We should never give up. We will never know what we gave up when we give up. It is through faith and patient endurance that people inherit God's promises. Therefore, we must stay the course and only change direction when it is clear we are on the wrong path.

14. **The Law of Attraction:** Each of us is a living magnet, attracting into our lives what we embody. To change what we are attracting, we must change who we are. We change who we are by changing our thinking. Changing our thinking is spiritual warfare requiring the weapons of our warfare (2 Corinthians 10: 3-5), which include the Word of God, the name of Jesus, and the blood of Jesus.

15. **The Law of Sowing and Reaping:** We may not reap where we sow, we may not reap when we sow, but we always reap what we sow. That is the law of sowing and

reaping. To earn more in life, you have to become more. To change the results we are getting in life, we have to pay the price in preparation and effort. In this life, you do not just wait; you should sow what you need the most, for it shall surely come back to you. For there is the person who withholds more than is necessary, and it leads to poverty rather than prosperity.

16. **The Law of Marriage:** For this cause, a man leaves his father and his mother and shall cleave to his wife, and the two shall become one flesh. That is the law of marriage. Marriage is the highest level of partnership in human relationships. People who cheat on their marriage partners cannot be trusted as business partners. But this is also the law of relationships. To succeed in marriage as in life, we must appreciate the uniqueness of each person and their gift.

17. **The Law of Acceptance:** In human relationships, we can be accepting of others and focus on their strengths rather than their weaknesses. In the law of acceptance, also known as the law of difference, you accept the uniqueness of each person but understand that no one is better than you. You play to your strength and focus on running in your lane while acknowledging others. You learn from everyone, but you do not compare yourself to anyone.

18. **The Law of Compounding:** According to Einstein, compound interest is the eighth wonder of the world. He who understands it, earns it ... he who doesn't ... pays it." Life on earth compounds. Future success is built on

existing success. We do not always have to start afresh. We must rely on residual knowledge to move forward.

19. **The Law of Focus:** According to Google's English dictionary, focus is the act of concentrating interest or activity on something. What does it mean to focus? It means to pay a lot of attention to a particular thing, to be undeterred and undistracted. When you focus on your focus, you will become a focus.

20. **The Law of Reproduction:** This is the law of Genesis. In Genesis everything created had fruit and was to reproduce after its kind. This is also the meaning of fruitfulness or being fruitful. We reproduce who we are, and we are called to reproduce what we are. God expects us to first be fruitful and then multiply so we do not multiply errors in society.

21. **The Law of Planning:** What is planning? Planning is allocating or assigning activities to time. If we fail to plan, we are planning to fail. Planning is also predetermining and predicting future events. Planning through creating schedules and following them is the primary way to take control of our lives and our time. In other words, we are to plan our work and work the plan.

22. **The Law of Sin:** Sin is missing the mark. All have missed the mark and must adjust their lives. The end result of sin is death. There is life after death. Throughout the Holy Scriptures death means separation but not cessation of existence. We will never cease to exist. We are spiritual beings. However, unless we are reconciled to our Maker and the Creator, who is God

through the vicarious work of Jesus on the cross, we will ultimately be eternally separated from God. This is called the second and final death (Revelation 20: 14-15).

23. **The Law of the Spirit:** Life on Earth is spiritual. We must take advantage of the spirit realm to make a difference in time. In order to experience the supernatural, we must trust and believe in a God of miracles. Everyone will need a miracle at some point in their life. As spiritual people, we walk by faith and not by sight (2 Corinthians 5:7). But without faith, it is impossible to please Him: for he that comes to God must believe that He is, and that He is a rewarder of them that diligently seek Him (Hebrews 11:6).

24. **Personal Transformation:** To transform means to change. The first law of transformation is first within, then without. Unless there is a change within, there can be no change without. The highest and most important level of transformation is not a transformation in location or transformation in your dressing, but a change in mindset. Unless your thoughts change, no real change has taken place.

CHAPTER 1

LAWS OF THE UNIVERSE
AND LIFE PLANNING

Someone might ask, "Why should I plan my life in the first place?" or "Why should anyone even attempt to organize their life?" These are valid questions, considering the fact that most of the over seven billion people currently residing on Earth are still searching for and grappling with the meaning of life. Therefore, planning our lives may be considered far-fetched. However, there are several reasons we should plan our lives.

Firstly, life on Earth is like a vapor that appears for a little time and then vanishes away.

James 4:14

"Whereas ye know not what shall be on the morrow. For what is your life? It is even a vapour, that appeareth for a little time, and then vanisheth away.

In other words, life on Earth at best is short. Unfortunately, we also have no spare life. We must therefore be careful to number our days and apply our hearts to wisdom. The main way to number our days is by planning them.

Secondly, man was created in the image of God and in God's likeness. Being created in the image of God implies that we were made as God's replica. God duplicated Himself in mankind. And not only did God create us in His image, but He also created us after His likeness, which means we were created to function like God. We have the ability of God. That is, we have God-like abilities. Planning is an ability of God. God is a meticulous planner.

Thirdly, not only did mankind receive God-given ability in the Garden of Eden where life on earth began, but the Bible also states in Genesis 1: 28 that God blessed man. With that blessing came other things. God blessed man with enormous potential and capacity, including the ability to plan. Planning is forecasting the future. For example, planning is an ability of God that resides only in mankind. There is no other creature on earth that has this ability. Neither goats, nor lions, nor zebras can plan.

The fourth reason we must plan is that research and studies have shown that the primary way to harness the enormous potential which is resident in humans is by organizing and structuring our lives. [1]Mark McCormack, a wildly successful entrepreneur and founder of the International Management Group, describes a study conducted on Harvard MBA's in 1979 in his book, "*What They Don't Teach You at Harvard Business School.* The study simply asked these MBA's: "Have you set clear, written goals for your future and made plans to

---

[1]https://www.linkedin.com/pulse/what-top-3-harvard-mbas-did-become-rich-you-can-do-too-dan-stern/November 11, 2015

accomplish them?" Sounds simple enough, right? The study found that: 84% of these students didn't have specific goals; 13% of the MBA's did have goals but didn't have any formal method of committing to them; only 3% had clear, written goals with a plan to accomplish them. Guess which group had to make the most bank runs with cash falling out of their pockets? (Hint: not the 84% with no specific goals). The researchers interviewed the students from this graduating class again in 1989, and found staggering results. The 13% with softly committed goals were earning twice as much as the 84% with no goals at all. But, the real winners from that graduating class were, you guessed it, the top 3% who had clear, written goals; they took home ten times as much as the other 97% of their class combined." While this story might have been refuted, the message is clear.

The lesson from this study is that taking time to see into the future, which is applying the laws of thought and vision, writing goals, which is applying the law of goals, taking the time to plan, which is applying the laws of time and planning, and deciding to follow your clearly written goals, which is applying the laws of action and decision, and actually staying the course, which is applying the law of persistence, will have a monumental impact on the outcome of your life. We cannot maximize the enormous potential in our lives without harnessing our inner resources through planning.

A fifth reason we must plan is simply because the primary way we can leave a legacy in this lifetime and leave our footprints on the sand of time is by planning. Planning is one of the laws of the Universe. Consider Samson, one of the Judges of Israel in the Old Testament of the Christian Bible. His birth was announced by an Angel. His mother supernaturally received specific instructions on how Samson was supposed to live his life. In his teenage years, Samson had supernatural encounters (Judges 13: 25). We learn from the life of Samson that every role in life has rules. Even though Samson was called as a deliverer to the nation of Israel, ultimately, he killed more people the day he died than in all the days of his life. "So, the dead whom he slew at his death were more than those whom he slew in his life (Judges 16: 30b)." Why? This is either because Samson did not plan his life, or he did not follow the plan. Samson lived a life of contradictions and violated some of the rules associated with his God-given role. Samson failed to be decisive on how he wanted to be remembered. Unlike Samson, Joseph produced a different kind of result. Joseph had personal discipline, and the Lord was with him; he prospered even in prison (Genesis 39:2, 20-23). Joseph lived in obedience and fear of God, warding off the temptations from Potiphar's wife (Genesis 39:7-12), and died at the age of one hundred and ten years (Genesis 50: 26). By faith, Joseph, when he died, made mention of the departure of the children of Israel; and gave commandments concerning his bones (Hebrews 11: 22). Just like Joseph, Alfred Nobel was a Swedish chemist, inventor, engineer, entrepreneur, and businessman who wrote poetry and drama. He is most remembered for inventing dynamite, his most famous invention, an explosive using nitroglycerin, which was patented in 1867. As a result of a popular story about how, in 1888, Nobel was astonished to read his own obituary, titled "The Merchant of Death Is Dead", in a French newspaper, Alfred Nobel literally rewrote his own obituary.

A sixth reason we must plan our lives is so we can live systematically. One of the laws of the Universe is the Law of Systems. The Law of Systems states that whatever is not systematic is not sustainable. This is part of the challenge that Samson faced. To live systematically, you have to build the system. Building systems requires discipline, and living by systems requires restraint. According to Adelaja "There is no reason to do anything if you do not make it a system!" This is because Adelaja believes 75% of success is in creating a system, and 25% of success is in following a system. I agree with Adelaja. Life planning is a way to live out our priorities. Life planning empowers us to build our lives in such a way that we can reach our goals and purpose every day.

Life planning is more than just setting goals and making to-do lists; it's about aligning our actions, thoughts, and aspirations with the profound wisdom that underlies the cosmos. These universal principles help us in our personal growth and give us fulfillment - from the Law of Thought, which emphasizes the power of our beliefs and mindset, to the Law of Persistence, which reminds us of the importance of resilience and determination. By integrating these laws into our life planning process, we not only navigate challenges with grace and confidence, but it helps us understand how we can make the most of our lives.

1. The Law of Thought: Before embarking on any life plan, it's essential to examine and align our thoughts with our desired outcomes. By cultivating a positive and growth-oriented mindset, we lay a solid foundation for setting and achieving our life goals.

2. The Law of Goals: Life planning revolves around setting clear, specific, measurable, achievable, realistic, and time-bound (SMART) goals. These goals provide direction, motivation, and a roadmap for our journey through life.

3. The Law of Words: The words we use shape our reality. In life planning, it's crucial to choose words that empower and inspire us towards our goals. By speaking positively about our aspirations and affirming our capabilities, we reinforce our commitment to success.

4. The Law of Time: Time is a limited resource, and effective life planning requires us to prioritize and allocate our time wisely. By recognizing the value of time and managing it efficiently, we maximize our productivity and progress toward our life goals.

5. The Law of Purpose: Understanding our purpose gives meaning and direction to our life planning efforts. By clarifying our values, passions, and long-term objectives, we can tailor our plans to align with our unique purpose and vision for the future.

6. The Law of Vision or Visualization: Visualization techniques can be powerful tools in life planning. By mentally rehearsing our desired outcomes and envisioning ourselves achieving our goals, we strengthen our belief in our ability to succeed and overcome obstacles along the way.

7. The Law of Faith: Belief in ourselves and our ability to manifest our dreams is essential in life planning. By cultivating faith and confidence in our capabilities, we approach challenges with resilience and determination, knowing that success is within reach.

8. The Law of Prayer: Prayer or meditation can be valuable practices in life planning. By connecting with our inner selves or connecting ourselves to God we gain clarity, guidance, and strength to pursue our life goals with purpose and integrity.

9. The Law of Action: Life planning requires proactive steps toward our goals. By taking consistent and purposeful action, we turn our aspirations into reality and move closer to realizing our goals in life.

10. The Law of Systems: Establishing effective systems and routines support our life planning efforts. By creating habits, processes, and structures that streamline our actions and decisions, we enhance our efficiency and productivity over time.

11. The Law of Conversion: Time management skills are crucial in life planning. By converting our time into productive activities, such as learning, creating, or building relationships, we make meaningful progress towards our life goals.

12. The Law of Decisions: Life planning involves making intentional decisions that align with our values and priorities. By decisively committing to our goals and taking responsibility for our actions, we empower ourselves to shape our destiny.

13. The Law of Persistence: Persistence is key to overcoming obstacles and setbacks in life planning. By staying committed to our goals and persevering through challenges, we build resilience and fortitude to weather any storm.

14. The Law of Attraction: Positive thoughts and energy attract opportunities and resources in life planning. By maintaining a mindset of abundance and possibility, we attract favorable outcomes.

15. The Law of Sowing and Reaping: Life planning involves investing in our growth and development over time. By sowing seeds of effort, discipline, and perseverance, we reap the rewards of personal and professional fulfillment.

16. The Law of Marriage: Building strong relationships and partnerships is integral to life planning. By nurturing trust, communication, and mutual respect in your marriage and profession, you create a supportive network that propels you towards your goals.

17. The Law of Acceptance: Embracing ourselves and others with compassion and understanding is essential in life planning. By accepting our strengths and weaknesses, we cultivate self-awareness and authenticity, fostering growth and resilience.

18. The Law of Compounding: Consistent effort and incremental progress lead to significant results in life planning. By leveraging the power of compounding, we amplify our achievements and create a legacy of success over time.

19. The Law of Focus: Concentrating our energy and attention on our priorities accelerates progress in life planning. By eliminating distractions and staying focused on our goals, we increase our effectiveness and achieve greater outcomes.

20. The Law of Reproduction: Living by example and embodying our values inspires others in life planning. By modeling integrity, passion, and purpose, we influence and empower those around us to pursue their own aspirations.

21. The Law of Planning: Strategic planning lays the groundwork for success in life planning. By setting clear objectives, developing actionable strategies, and adapting to changing circumstances, we navigate life's challenges with confidence and purpose.

22. The Law of Sin: Acknowledging our shortcomings and learning from our mistakes is essential in life planning. By embracing humility and accountability, we cultivate resilience and wisdom to overcome obstacles and grow from adversity.

23. The Law of the Spirit: Connecting with our spiritual beliefs and values enriches our life planning journey. By seeking guidance, inspiration, and strength from our spiritual practices, we find solace and purpose amidst life's uncertainties.

24. Personal Transformation: Embracing change and growth is foundational to life planning. By continually evolving our mindset, skills, and perspectives, we unlock new opportunities and unleash our full potential in pursuit of our life goals.

In addition to figures like Alfred Nobel, Paul the Apostle, Benjamin Franklin, and Richard L. Kramer, this book builds on the lives and works of a few other men including Abraham

Maslow, Peter J. Daniel, Alan Lakein, Richard Winwood, Warren Buffet, and Sunday Adelaja.

CHAPTER 2

UNDERSTANDING THE LAW OF TIME

Genesis 1:1 – NKJV
"In the beginning, God created the heavens and the earth."

Genesis 1:1 - NCV
1 "In the beginning, God created the sky and the earth."

The phrase "In the beginning" in the above passage refers to the beginning of time and creation. God, who has no beginning, started the work of creation by creating the beginning, which was the beginning of time. He created the sky or the heavens, which is space or outer space, and the earth, which is matter.

We all struggle with the concept of time. Understanding the concept of time is both fascinating and frustrating. It seems to fly by in the blink of an eye, yet sometimes stretches out endlessly. The Law of Time reminds us that time is a limited and limiting resource – the very essence of life itself. But where did this concept originate, what are its characteristics, and how can we harness its power throughout our lives?

What is Time?
While we all experience time, defining it can be surprisingly tricky. Let us explore different ways to understand this fundamental concept.

Linear Progression: Time is often described as a linear flow, with events unfolding from the past to the present and into the future.

Measurement and Units: We measure time using units like seconds, minutes, hours, and years, creating a framework for organizing our lives.

Perception: Our perception of time can be subjective. Time seems to slow down during moments of intense focus or excitement, while mundane tasks can make hours feel like an eternity.

According to Isaac Newton, time is absolute. It occurs whether the universe is here or not. Leibniz, a German scientist, describes time as merely the order of events, and not an entity in itself. Albert Einstein said time has no independent existence by itself except the events by which it is measured.

According to Webster's Dictionary of English, time is a continuum in which events succeed themselves from past, present, to the future.

How do you define time?

What is your personal definition of time? How do you use your time? What do you do with your time? Can you account for your time? Can you account for the last week of your life? What about the last month? How old are you? What have you really done with your life? In my book, "*Understanding the Laws of the Universe: Enduring Principles for Building and Maximizing Life on Earth*", I define time as an interval and a pause in the continuum called eternity. God created time to create life and to dimension life on earth. God lives in a different dimension called eternity, which is infinite. One day, time will be up, and God will fold time and put it away the way you fold your clothing and put it in your wardrobe.

What are the characteristics of time?

Time has unique characteristics that should influence how we approach life:

1. **Irreversible**: One key characteristic of time is that it cannot be reversed. We cannot rewind time or fast forward through life. This characteristic emphasizes the importance of living in the present moment and making the most of every opportunity.

2. **Relativity**: Albert Einstein's theory of relativity showed that time can be perceived differently depending on an observer's motion and location. While the concept is complex, it highlights the subjective nature of time perception.

3. **Involuntary:** If you consider time as the fourth dimension, with others being length, width, and height, time can be said to be involuntary or unstoppable. Although the Earth and the Milky Way are in constant motion, you can stop at a point on the Earth, but you cannot do the same with time. Time is in constant motion

and cannot be stopped.

4. **Irretrievable:** Each person can think of lost time, which is usually equated to lost opportunity. Time once lost cannot be recovered. This is why we talk about seizing the opportunity in the lifetime of that opportunity.

5. **Time cannot be saved:** Time is in constant motion. We therefore have no control over time. Once we get our daily quota of 24 hours, time is in constant motion. Time will pass itself, sixty seconds every minute, and sixty minutes every hour. All we can do is to gain understanding and adapt ourselves. You either waste it, spend it, or invest it in some profitable and productive activity. Since you cannot stop the passage of time, you cannot save time.

6. **Time cannot be stopped:** Time is in constant motion. You can pause your clock or your watch, but you cannot stop the flow of time. As a result of the constant flow of time, most people on Earth are playing catch with time and their God-ordained purpose.

Where did Time come from?

Time, space, and matter were created simultaneously by God. In my book Understanding the Laws of the Universe: Enduring Principles for Building and Maximizing Life on Earth, I state that "The first thing God created was time, which was the beginning of creation. When the Bible says, "In the Beginning", it is referring to two things: the beginning of time and the beginning of creation." This is because God created time to start the work of creation and to dimension life on Earth. In other words, God created time to create life. Mathematically speaking, if time is represented by the letter 'T' and life is represented by the letter 'L", then

T = L

Time is therefore life. Where did time come from? Time is an earthly phenomenon and a different dimension of measurement compared to God who is eternal. Eternity is infinite and a continuum. Time will not always exist. Time had a beginning and will eventually come to an end. Time was the first thing God created. This age or dispensation will eventually come to an end.

What is the Law of Time?

Time is life. It is a limited and controlling resource. Every day God credits all humans alive with 24 hours, which is 86,400 seconds. No one can have more, but you can achieve more with your time. You can create more value with your time. One must obey and follow the law of conversion. The laws of the Universe are interrelated and interdependent. The law of time states that all things are created in time and all things are subject to time.

What do you do with your time?

The Law of Time emphasizes that how you use your time determines the quality of your life. Are you frittering away precious moments on mindless activities, or are you investing your time in pursuits that bring you closer to your goals and dreams? What do you do with your time? How do you use time? There are only three things you can do with time. You can waste, spend, or invest your time. You have wasted time when you cannot account for it. You spend time when your time is controlled by others or circumstances. You invest your time when you use your time to fulfill your purpose for existence. Anything you do with time that is not contributing to your purpose for existence is not time well used. Everyone can look back in time and recognize that they have lost time. Making the most of life is not trying to recover lost time; rather, it is maximizing your remaining days on earth. You maximize your days by considering how little time you have left, running faster, being more accountable for your time, and by making the most of your remaining time. You make the most of your remaining time by maximizing the seconds. You cannot maximize your seconds unless you have discovered and documented your reason for existence. You make the most of your seconds by creating schedules based on goals and making yourself a slave to those schedules. To maximize time, you need to seize every opportunity and stop making excuses or idling away your life.

Lessons from Benjamin Franklin

Benjamin Franklin can be described as a time management guru, and he was also a champion of personal productivity.

Mastering Time

According to Dr. David Ogbueli, in his book, *The Secrets of Self-Improvement from the Life of Benjamin Franklin:*
"Franklin had strong opinions about time: how to best use it, what not to do with time, and the true value of time. Benjamin Franklin understood three important things about time.

1. Firstly, time is the one thing that, when lost, can never be recovered.
2. Secondly, time is necessary and a necessity for all else in this world. Everything on earth is subject to the law of time, and everything is a product of time.
3. Thirdly, for most people, time is their most squandered and most wasted resource, and the full value of time is something they never fully understand or appreciate."

Franklin understood time. He comprehended that time was both a limiting and controlling resource.

Ogbueli surmises that Franklin understood that:
"Quite literally, time is money and time is life; therefore, time must be considered the most precious thing that we own. Yet the wonderful thing about time is that we have total and complete control over how it's used. We can decide to apply our precious time to being productive or watch it evaporate like the dew from a morning flower. To master time is to take full and deliberate control over your entire life. It's our choice. You can resolve to be the master of your time."

The Law of Time in Action: How Time Shapes Our Lives

The Law of Time dictates that time is a limited resource, the very essence of life itself. The law of time shapes and impacts our lives in the following ways:

1. Prioritization: Since time is limited, we need to prioritize tasks and activities that align with our goals and values.

2. Procrastination: Putting things off leads to wasted time and missed opportunities. Therefore, you should never leave until tomorrow what you need to do today.

3. Focus and Productivity: Effective time management allows us to focus on the important tasks and get more done in less time. We must deliberately live our lives in the quadrant of things that are important but not yet urgent.

What is a Timeline?

We all have a timeline. Each of our lives has a beginning, and our lives will expire one day. Between our birth and our death is our timeline, a graphical representation of our lives and important milestones. What are you doing with your time? How are you living your life? How will you be remembered? Lessons from history tell us that different people produce different results in their lives. For example, the Apostle Paul of Bible fame wrote most of the New Testament. There are twenty-seven books of the New Testament, and he undeniably authored thirteen of the twenty-seven books of the New Testament. How did he find time to accomplish so much? The apostle was not only an author but also traveled extensively throughout the New Testament era and went the furthest among his contemporaries, going as far as Rome. In his own words, "I labored more abundantly than them." How did he do it? His life was focused and planned. He was a visionary and persistent. The apostle was decisive and very determined. He had a sound mind and was goal-oriented. Paul, the apostle, was accustomed to following and obeying his purpose. He found his purpose, which was his particular lane in the grand scheme of things. The apostle was either single or separated, so he had sufficient time on his hands to get a lot done.

Let's consider the timeline of Paul the Apostle:

Birth & Education
A.D. 6 Born a Roman citizen to Jewish parents in Tarsus (in modern eastern Turkey)
20–30 Studied Torah in Jerusalem with Gamaliel; became a Pharisee
30–33 Persecuted followers of Jesus of Nazareth in Jerusalem and Judea
Conversion
33–36 Converted on the way to Damascus; spent three years in Arabia; returned to Damascus to preach Jesus as Messiah
36 Fled Damascus because of persecution; visited Jerusalem and met with the apostles
36–44 Preached in Tarsus and the surrounding regions.
44–46 Invited by Barnabas to teach in Antioch

46 With Barnabas visited Jerusalem to bring a famine relief offering.

Mission Trips

47–48 First missionary journey with Barnabas, to Cyprus and Galatia

49 At the Council of Jerusalem, Paul argued that Gentile Christians need not follow Jewish law; returned to Antioch; confronted Peter over the question of Jewish law.

49–52 Second missionary journey with Silas, through Asia Minor and Greece; settled in Corinth; wrote letters to the Thessalonians

52 Visited Jerusalem and Antioch briefly; began the third missionary journey.

52–55 Stayed in Ephesus; wrote the letters to the Galatians and Corinthians

55–57 Traveled through Greece and possibly Illyricum (modern Yugoslavia); wrote a letter to the Romans

Arrest & Death

57–59 Returned to Jerusalem and was arrested; imprisoned at Caesar-ea

59–60 Appeared before Festus and appealed to Caesar; voyage to Rome

60–62 Under house arrest in Rome; wrote letters to the Philippians, Ephesians, Colossians, and Philemon

62–64 Released; journeyed to Spain; wrote letters to Timothy and Titus

64 Returned to Rome; martyred during persecution.

Paul lived an accomplished life. He achieved so much in one lifetime. At the end of his life, he was able to say, 'I have finished my course,' which was his heartfelt cry. Paul was an author who penned down a significant portion of the New Testament, a missionary who traveled the then-known world, a church planter who had the care of many churches, a city taker who shook cities to their roots, a trainer of men and women who led an army of disciples, and a nation builder who laid the foundation of Europe on the principles of God's word, known as the old world, among many other things.

What is your timeline?

How are you living your life? How will you be remembered? Are you happy? Are you satisfied with life? Are you fulfilled? Do you need to make changes in your life?

Lessons from Alfred Bernhard Nobel

Alfred Nobel was born on October 21st, 1833 and passed away on December 10th, 1896. He was a Swedish chemist, inventor, engineer, entrepreneur, and businessman who wrote poetry and drama. He is most remembered for inventing dynamite, his most famous invention, an explosive using nitroglycerin, which was patented in 1867. There is a popular story about how, in 1888, Nobel was astonished to read his own obituary, titled "The Merchant of Death Is Dead", in a French newspaper. However, it was actually Alfred's brother Ludwig who had died; the obituary was eight years premature. The article disconcerted Nobel and made him apprehensive about how he would be remembered. This inspired him to change his will. Though historians have been unable to verify this story, and others dismiss it as a myth, on December 10th, 1896, Alfred Nobel eventually died in his villa in San Reno, Italy, from a cerebral hemorrhage at age 63. In his last will, Nobel specified that his fortune be used to create a series of prizes for those who confer the "greatest benefit on mankind" in the areas of physics, chemistry, physiology or medicine, literature, and peace. He bequeathed 94% of his total assets, 31 million SEK (approximately US$186 million, €150 million in 2008), to establish the five Nobel Prizes.

As a result of skepticism surrounding the will, it was not approved until April 26th, 1897. Ragnarök Holman and Rudolf Liljenquist, the Executors of the will, formed the Nobel Foundation to take care of the fortune and to organize the awarding of prizes.

Writing Your Own Obituary

The lesson we learn from Alfred Nobel is that we can write our own obituary. Mr. Nobel had the unfortunate but unique opportunity of reading his own obituary, which was eight years premature. He decided to change the narrative and to determine how he would be remembered. He rewrote his will so many times and eventually landed on his last will, which is how he is remembered today as the initiator of the Nobel Prizes, which have literally changed the world. Each of us can predetermine how we will be remembered.

Is it possible to take control of time?
According to the Holy Scriptures, "In the beginning, God created the heavens and the earth." In the beginning, the beginning of what? It refers to the beginning of the work of creation and the creation of the earth. In starting the work of creation, the first thing God created was time. There could have been no beginning without time. He who lives outside of time started the work of creation by creating time so that He could dimension life on earth. God created time to initiate the work of creation. He created time to bring life on Earth. Therefore, mathematically speaking, time equates to life. Your time represents your life. You measure life on Earth by time. You manage your life by managing and controlling your time. What you do with your time is what you have done with your life. You need to mind the gap of time.

As an individual, your most valuable resource is your time, which is constantly in motion. Every day, God allots every person living on Earth with 86,400 seconds, which must elapse by the close of the day. You absolutely cannot stop the flow of time. You cannot stop or capture time. Time once lost cannot be recovered. Benjamin Franklin said, "Do you love life? Then don't squander time, for that is the stuff life is made of."

But is it possible to take control of your time? The answer is yes! Though we cannot control time, you can control your own time. Control starts with planning. Since time is a limited resource, the only way we can maximize our life is by taking control of our limited time. The way we take control is by planning. Fundamentally, planning is predetermining future events. Planning is one of the laws of the universe.

CHAPTER 3

THE CASE FOR PLANNING

I have been a Christian for more than thirty years. One of the struggles and challenges for people of faith is the apparent conflict between planning for the future and Spirit-led living.

Jeremiah 10:23
O Lord, I know that **the way of man is not in himself;** *it* **is not in man** *who walks to direct his steps.*

Jeremiah 10:23 - NKJV
O Lord, I know the way of man is not in himself; **It is not in man who walks to direct his own steps.**

What does this passage mean? When the Bible states that the way of man is not in himself, what does it mean? The passage states further that the man who walks cannot direct himself. What does that really mean? We must compare scripture with scripture. The emphasis of the passage in this case is on the sovereignty of God. This implies that our lives are not entirely in our hands. It is possible to interpret the above passage to mean that we should not plan, since the way of man is not in himself. However, that passage really means you will never have a plan for your life better than the plan God has for you. Some might still ask, "Why should we plan?"

Why Should We Plan?

If only God's plan or counsel will come to pass, is it still necessary to plan? In other words, why should we plan when ultimately God's plan will come to pass? Planning is predetermining future events. It is the primary way we take control of our lives by controlling how we spend our time. For spiritual people, the key question is: Who is in charge? Is God in charge of your life, or are you in charge of your life? Is it spiritual to plan? What about scriptures like:

Proverbs 19: 20-21
20 Hear counsel, and receive instruction, that thou mayest be wise in thy latter end. 21 There are many devices in a man's heart; nevertheless, the counsel of the Lord, that shall stand.

Proverbs 19: 20-21 - NKJV
20 Listen to counsel and receive instruction, That you may be wise in your latter days. 21 There are many plans in a man's heart; nevertheless, the counsel of the Lord, that shall stand.

The word translated "device" in the King James Version in Proverbs 19: 21 means "plans" as seen in the New King James Version. This passage means that we may have many plans, but only God's counsel will ultimately come to pass. To understand the passage further, we must compare scripture with scripture. Superficially, we could interpret Proverbs 19; 21 as meaning we should not plan because only God's counsel will stand. However, let's look at a few other scriptures in the Christian Bible.

Psalm 37:4

4 Delight yourself also in the Lord: and he shall give you the desires of your heart. 5 Commit your way unto the Lord; trust also in him, and he shall bring it to pass.

Proverbs 16:1-3

1 The preparations of the heart in man, and the answer of the tongue, are from the Lord. 2 All the ways of a man are clean in his own eyes, but the Lord weighs the spirits. 3 Commit your works unto the Lord, and your thoughts shall be established. "

God Reveals His Plan Through Our Desires

In Psalm 37: 4, when the desires of your heart are written down on paper, they become your plans and your way. The word 'commit' in both Psalm 37:4 and Proverbs 16: 3 means to *roll on the LORD your plans, thoughts, or works*. The word 'preparations' in Proverbs 16:1 means plans. Therefore, the phrase 'preparations of the heart in man' means 'plans of man, which are in his heart'. The phrase 'the answer of the tongue is from the Lord means the counsel of the Lord shall stand or the plans of the Lord will come to pass. Essentially, it means the plans of God shall stand. What the Bible is implying is that God will work through our desires, especially as we roll them over unto Him." In other words, God will give us a peek into His future plans and share with us how He is thinking about the future through the desires He places within us. The desires in our hearts are God's thoughts about the future placed in our hearts, and as we wait on God, especially as we roll these desires over to the Lord. God will ultimately cause them to materialize and come to pass. Planning is a function only available to mankind. There is no other creature created by God that is capable of planning.

Whose Business Is It To Make The Earth Work?

Genesis 1:26
26 And God said, "Let us make man in our image, after our likeness, and let them have dominion over the fish of the sea, and over the fowl of the air, and over the cattle, and over all the earth, and over every creeping thing that creepeth upon the earth."

In Genesis 1: 26, God said, "Let *us and let them."* That is a big deal! This is the cultural and dominion mandate. Whose business is it to make the nations work? Who should make disciples of nations? Who is responsible for running the government of the nations? Who is in charge of your business, shop, or your school, or medical practice? If you want to get more practical, you could ask, who built the United States of America? Who built the Coca-Cola company? Who built Microsoft Corporation? Who built Amazon? Who built Facebook? In each case, the answer is man. Even though there is a partnership between God and man, and an interplay of divinity and humanity, God has given the earth to mankind.

Psalm 115:16 - NKJV

16 The heavens, even the heavens, are the Lord's; But the earth He has given to the children of men.

Psalm 115:16 - NIV

16 The highest heavens belong to the Lord, but the earth he has given to mankind.

Interplay of Humanity and Divinity

As a result of the above passages, man is responsible for the earth. God gave the Earth to humankind. If God gave the earth to mankind, whose responsibility is it to run the earth? Who is supposed to till and cultivate the earth? When this earth fails, who should be blamed? So, if man is responsible for the earth, and the key to control is planning, and planning is a key management function, who should plan how the earth should run?

If you don't work, you shouldn't eat.

We already know that the man who will not work should not eat. Therefore, you must plan your work and work the plan. If you do not plan your work and therefore do not work, Paul the apostle admonished that you should not eat. Therefore, it is an interplay between humanity and divinity.

2 Thessalonians 3:10 - NKJV
10 For even when we were with you, we commanded you this: If anyone will not work, neither shall he eat.

Prayer and Planning

Let's consider the need and case for prayer. [2]Evangelist Asa Alonso Allen (March 27, 1911 – June 11, 1970), better known as A. A. Allen, was an American Pentecostal evangelist known for his faith healing and deliverance ministry. He was, for a time, associated with the "Voice of Healing" movement founded by Gordon Lindsay. Many years ago Evangelist Alonzo Asa Allen wrote in the classic book *The Price of God's Miracle Working Power*, reintroduced by Evangelist R. W. Shambach, that "Real prayer -- determined, prevailing prayer -- is the greatest outlet of power on earth." Allen was right, and I completely agree with him. However, when should we pray and how should we pray? Anyone who doubts the potency of prayer may not have a personal experience with prayer. In John 14:13, Jesus said, "And whatsoever you shall ask the Father in my name, that will I do." In John 14: 14, Jesus said further, "If you shall ask anything in my name, I will do *it.*"

The Answered Prayer

John 14:12-14 - NKJV
12 "Most assuredly, I say to you, he who believes in Me, the

---

2 https://en.wikipedia.org/wiki/A. A. Allen, lasted edited on July 28, 2024 by 4;28 (UTC)

works that I do he will do also; and greater works than these he will do because I go to My Father. 13 And whatever you ask in My name, that I will do, so that the Father may be glorified in the Son. 14 If you ask anything in My name, I will do it.

The passage above emphasizes the possibilities of prayer. In fact, in John 14: 14, the word '*it*' is italicized, meaning there is no limit to what God can do in response to requests made in the name of God. In the original writing and language, the implication is that if you ask Jesus for anything that does not currently exist, Jesus will provide for you. That is powerful! In my book *The Possibilities of Prayer*, I share the story of forgetting my handset in a restroom at Sandton Mall in South Africa and recovering my handset by prayer.

³Lesson from South Africa

Just recently, I was visiting South Africa, in the city of Sandton. One day, while at Sandton City Mall, I left my phone in the public restroom. The challenge was that a significant amount of time had passed before I remembered that I left my phone in the restroom, which posed a challenge. I was already in another shop when I came to myself and remembered that I had forgotten my phone in the restroom. More than twenty minutes could have elapsed. I found my way back to the restroom, but the particular room I had used was occupied. What should I do? What would you have done if you were in my situation? In a case like this, in the past, I

---

3 Enelamah, John C., *The Possibilities of Prayer*, JEM Publishing 2021, pg. 18

would have been totally confused. However, in this case, although I had a sense of loss, I refrained from accepting the idea of permanently losing my phone. Though I panicked briefly, I remained composed. I definitely did not want to misplace the handset, as it was a crucial tool for work while on the move. It was only three months old and served other functions for the ministry, including acting as a video camera.

Through prayer, specifically the Prayer of Decree and Controlling Prayers, I recovered my phone. Therefore, I acknowledge that prayer is highly potent and effective. Nevertheless, does the effectiveness and the potential of prayer imply that we should not plan? We need to ask the question, is prayer an end in itself or a means to an end. In other words, when is the appropriate time to pray? Is there a time to stop praying? Is there a time not to pray at all? Put another way, when ought we to pray? When should we cease praying? And when should we not pray at all?

Typology in the Bible

The New Testament is concealed in the Old and the Old is revealed in the New. The above statement, credited to Saint Augustine is a way of describing the relationship between the Old and New Testaments of the Bible. In other words, the substance lies within the New Testament, while the shadow resides in the Old Testament. According to David and Susan

Sifford, [4]"There are two components in the Bible called "type" and "anti-type" (collectively referred to as "typology"). Types, or shadows, are spiritual "pictures" shown in the Bible that symbolize concepts or individuals. The fulfillment of a type is referred to as its "anti-type."" In the Bible, a type is a person, thing, or event in the Old Testament that foreshadows a corresponding person, thing, or event in the New Testament.

God is a God of Covenant

Genesis 15: 18-21

18 In the same day, the Lord made a covenant with Abram, saying, "Unto thy seed have I given this land, from the river of Egypt unto the great river, the river Euphrates: 19 The Kenites, and the Kenizzites, and the Kadmonites, 20 And the Hittites, and the Perizzites, and the Rephaims, 21 And the Amorites, and the Canaanites, and the Girgashites, and the Jebusites.

In Genesis God entered into a covenant with Abram, saying, "Unto thy seed have I given this land, from the river of Egypt unto the great river, the river Euraphates. By "thy seed," God was referring to the descendants of Abraham.

Numbers 33:51-55

---

[4]https://www.siffordsojournal.com/2009/09/davids-digest-introduction-to-type-and-antitype-typology-in-bible, Updated: Thursday, 07/20/2023 - 06:04

51 Speak unto the children of Israel, and say unto them, "When you have passed over the Jordan into the land of Canaan; 52 Then you shall drive out all the inhabitants of the land from before you, and destroy all their pictures, and destroy all their molten images, and completely pull down all their high places: 53 And you shall dispossess the inhabitants of the land and dwell therein, for I have given you the land to possess it" (Emphasis mine). 54 And you shall divide the land by lot for an inheritance among your families: to the more you shall give the more inheritance, and to the fewer you shall give the less inheritance: every man's inheritance shall be in the place where his lot falls; according to the tribes of your fathers you shall inherit. 55 But if you do not drive out the inhabitants of the land from before you, then it shall come to pass that those which you let remain of them shall be pricks in your eyes, and thorns in your sides, and shall vex you in the land wherein you dwell.

In Numbers God repeated the promise to Moses, *"for I have given you the land to possess it."* However, God reminded Moses, "you *shall dispossess the inhabitants of the land, and dwell therein:"*

Psalm 105: 7-11

7 He is the Lord our God: his judgments are in all the earth. 8 He has remembered his covenant forever, the word which he commanded to a thousand generations. 9 Which covenant he made with Abraham, and his oath to Isaac;

¹⁰ And confirmed the same to Jacob for a law, and to Israel for an everlasting covenant: ¹¹ Saying, unto thee will I give the land of Canaan, the lot of your inheritance."

In Psalm 105, God reminded the Israelites through David the Psalmist of the "covenant He made with Abraham, the oath with Isaac, which he confirmed unto Jacob for a law, and to Israel for an everlasting covenant."

The Promised Land was Occupied Territory

In Numbers God said to Moses specifically, *"for I have given you the land to possess it."* In other words, it was time to fulfill my covenant with Abraham. The question is, how were the children of Israel to fulfill the promise of possessing the Canaan land as was promised to Abraham? If God gave the Canaan land to the children of Israel, should they roll over and wait for God to deliver the land to them? If God gave a prophecy to Jeremiah, "before you came out of your mother's womb, I separated you and ordained you as a prophet to the nations." What should Jeremiah do?

Despite the fact that God entered into a covenant with Abraham, swearing an oath to Isaac, which He confirmed to Jacob as a law, and to Israel as an everlasting covenant, saying, "Unto thee will I give the land of Canaan as the lot of their inheritance," God still expected the children of Israel not only to fight for the Promised Land, but also to dispossess the inhabitants of the land through victorious battle. Though it was the promised land, it was still occupied territory.

Planning is Foreshadowed in the Old Testament

The lesson from God's dealings with Abraham illustrates to us the important principle of planning. Though God makes promises to us and answers our prayers, giving us a preview of that which is to come, we are to settle down to plan and map out that future and also take decisive actions to make the plan come to pass. This principle of planning is foreshadowed or prefigured in the Old Testament as typology. Though God is with us, we are not to go to war, write an examination, build a ministry or business, or even live our lives without proper planning. God is meticulous, so should we be. We are to count the cost and make plans before embarking on any venture. However, we must be decisive and action-oriented, knowing that nothing will happen until we make it happen.

Planning Despite the Superiority of God's Plan

Jeremiah 29: 11
For I know the thoughts that I think toward you, saith the Lord, thoughts of peace, and not of evil, to give you an expected end.

Jeremiah 29: 11 CEB

I know the plans I have in mind for you, declares the Lord; they are plans for peace, not disaster, to give you a future filled with hope.

Jeremiah 29: 11 CSB

For I know the plans I have for you"—this is the Lord's declaration— "plans for your well-being, not for disaster, to give you a future and a hope.

Jeremiah 29: 11 AMP

For I know the plans and thoughts that I have for you,' says the Lord, 'plans for peace and well-being and not for disaster, to give you a future and a hope.

In Jeremiah 29: 11, God is saying He has plans for our lives. When God says that His counsel will stand, in essence, He is saying we can never have or produce plans superior or better than the plans He has for us. We are to plan by rolling our desires onto the Lord and He will plan through us. How does God fine-tune our plans? By screening our plans and adjusting our plans.

Why Did God Forbid Paul?

In Acts 16: 6-7 Paul attempted to go into Asia and Bithynia, but the Holy Spirit forbade him. Was Paul being led by the Spirit or did he just go? If Paul was not led, why did he go? Wasn't Paul the Apostle sent out in Acts 13? Weren't we commanded to go into all the world and preach the gospel to every creature? Didn't Jesus commission His disciples to make disciples of all nations? Was Paul ambitious or out of sync with God? Can a Christian just get up and go? These questions revolve around purpose, planning, and divine timing. What Paul was likely dealing with was divine timing. Just like Moses the deliverer who lived thousands of years before Paul, Paul was probably sensing in his heart that there was work to be done in Asia. And yet, there was the timing factor. We know later Paul will be greatly used by God in Asia, where he probably spent the longest years of ministry in any one region.

Understanding Divine Timing

Acts 19:1-10
1 And it came to pass that, while Apollos was at Corinth, Paul having passed through the upper coasts, came to Ephesus: and found certain disciples. 2 He said unto them, "Have you received the Holy Ghost since you believed?" And they said unto him, "We have not so much as heard whether there is any Holy Ghost. 3 And he said unto them, "Unto what then were you baptized?" And they said, "Unto John's baptism." 4 Then said Paul, John indeed baptized with the baptism of repentance, saying unto the people that they should believe in him who should come after him, that is, Christ Jesus. 5 When they heard this, they were baptized in the name of the Lord Jesus. 6 And when Paul had laid his hands upon them, the Holy Ghost came upon them, and they spoke with

tongues and prophesied. 7 And all the men were about twelve. 8 And he went into the synagogue and spoke boldly for the space of three months, disputing and persuading the things concerning the kingdom of God. 9 But when some were hardened and did not believe, but spoke evil of the way before the multitude, he departed from them and separated the disciples, disputing daily in the school of one Tyrannus. 10 And this continued for the space of two years; so that all those who dwelt in Asia heard the word of the Lord Jesus, both Jews and Greeks.

The Whole of Asia Receives the Word

In the above passage in Acts 19, Paul having passed through the upper coasts, arrives at Ephesus. He ultimately ends up in the school of one Tyrannus after being kicked out of the synagogue. He is used so mightily by God including the working of special miracles, that according to Acts 19; 10, the whole of Asia receives the word of the Lord in the space of two years. However, this is the same Asia a few chapters and a few years before where Paul is prevented by the Holy Spirit from preaching the word. What is going on here? It has to do with how heaven views life on earth and timing.

How Does Heaven View Life?

How does Heaven view life on earth? Does God have a plan for each life? Can we have a peek into this plan? Can I find, focus on, follow, finish, and fulfill God's plan for my life? Is it possible to plan?" Can I plan the future? Maybe we can even take a step back and ask, does God have a purpose for our lives? Is there a reason why God created this earth? Does God have a specific plan for each life? When we study the lives of some of the greats according to documented history, we must ask how they accomplished so much in one lifetime. The question we must ask is, how can I fulfill my purpose? The lesson from history is that the greats in human history understood timing. Timing is everything.

Time is Everything

Have you ever heard the phrase, "time is everything." This is another lesson from Paul's ministry in Asia. Many times, we sense the leading of the Lord or a divine direction, but may not fully understand the timing and sequence of events. While we might be able to peek into the future through solitude, studying to be quiet, being sober, and praying, we cannot always understand the calendar of events and the timing of things, which God has reserved in His power. As a younger Christian this was a point of much confusion. In those days, there were many times when I sensed God's direction, but I also felt a restraint. It took many years, but I subsequently came to understand that it was a question of timing. A slight adjustment in timing can make a difference in planning and in a plan.

There Are Two Timings

There is another point about timing. Planning is allocating or assigning activities to time. There are usually two timings. There is divine timing and there is human timing. We may see events and activities in the future, but not in their proper sequence. God told Habakkuk the prophet, "If the vision tarries, wait for it, for it shall surely come; it shall not tarry." Is there a contradiction? If it tarries...it shall not tarry? Again, what is going on here? We are dealing with two timings: human timing and God's timing. When we plan, we might miss it according to human timing, but in God's time, every plan is beautiful and right on time. Timing is an integral part of planning.

Understanding God's Plan and His calendar

Acts 1: 6-7
6 When they therefore were come together, they asked of him, saying, Lord, wilt thou at this time restore again the kingdom to Israel? 7 And he said unto them, It is not for you to know the times or the seasons, which the Father hath put in his own power.

God has His own calendar. We therefore need to develop our personal calendar based on God's calendar. You need a plan for your life based on God's plan. God has a purpose for each of our lives, but that plan is a subset of His bigger plan. So, we plan, and our plans are subject to His plans.

What did Benjamin Franklin and Richard L. Kramer have in common?

For example, though separated by generations, Benjamin Franklin the framer of the US Constitution, and Richard L. Kramer of Nigerian business landscape fame, left their footprints on the sands of time. Though they now belong to the ages, their lives are full of accomplishments. What do they have in common? In my view, from researching their lives, the answer is *purposeful living* and *planning*. They both lived their lives in a systematic and predictable manner. Benjamin Franklin had his little book, to which he said, [5]"And it may well be that my posterity should be informed, that to this little artifice with the blessing of God their ancestor owed the constant felicity of his life down to his 79th year in which this is written." Dick Kramer had his MOGOS, to which he said Wanda, his wife, and himself owe their accomplishments. Both Benjamin Franklin and Dick Kramer planned and executed their lives. They were both deliberate and intentional. Neither Franklin nor Kramer mentioned or lived by New Year's resolutions. We learn the importance of life planning from their lives.

---

[5] Franklin, Benjamin, *The Autobiography of Benjamin Franklin*, Yale University Press 1964, p. 157

CHAPTER 4

UNDERSTANDING THE LAW
OF PLANNING

The Law of Time establishes time as a limited resource. But can we truly control something as seemingly elusive as time? While we cannot manipulate the flow of time itself, understanding the Law of Planning empowers us to manage it effectively. This chapter explores the concept of planning and how it allows us to prioritize tasks, reduce procrastination, and achieve our goals to help us make the most of life.

What is Planning?

Is it possible to take control of time? Can you take control of your life? How did people like Paul of the Bible fame achieve so much? What about Benjamin Franklin, a Framer of the US Constitution, and Richard L. Kramer of African Capital Alliance Nigeria? How did each of them accomplish so much in one lifetime? The key word is planning. According to Alan Lakein in his book *How to Get Control of Your Life and Your Time,* "the payoff in life is control of our life, and control starts with planning. To make the most of life, we have to take the driver's seat in managing our lives by sitting down to plan, create schedules, and make ourselves slaves to those schedules."

"In his classic book, *The Effective Executive*, the famous management consultant and theorist Peter F. Drucker suggests that the task of the time manager is to control time where he can. Alan Lakein, in his book *How To Get Control of Your Time and Your Life*, states that control is the key concept in time management." [6]"The primary way to control time is by planning. Man has the driver's seat on Earth. We are responsible for cultivating and tilling our Promised land. Mankind is responsible for ruling over the earth as God governs the Universe.

Why Should We Plan?

So, what should we do? We must realize that despite the fact that God's plan will come to pass, we as humans will need to go ahead and plan. We must remember that planning is a God-given ability given only to humans by God. Failing to plan is a plan in itself. So, why should we plan? If you do not plan, what are your options? Failing to plan is planning to fail. Ultimately, God's plan will come to pass. In Jeremiah 10: 23, we understand that the way of man is not in himself. But where is the way of man? It is in God, and God says, "Bring your plan or plans and let us reason together." We know that God's thoughts are not our thoughts, and God's ways are not our ways, but can God's thoughts and God's ways become our thoughts and our ways? The answer is yes! How?

---

[6] Winwood, Richard, I., *Time Management: An Introduction to the Franklin System,* Franklin International Institute, 1990, p. 5

The first thing we need to consider is that God wants us to accept responsibility for the earth. God gave this earth to mankind.

Psalm 115:16 - LB
16 *The heavens belong to the Lord, but he has given the earth to all mankind* (emphasis is mine).

Psalm 115:16 - NLT
16 *The heavens belong to the Lord, but he has given the earth to all humanity* (emphasis is mine).

The heavens belong to God, but God has given the earth to mankind and to humanity. God wants us to accept responsibility for the earth and for our lives. God gave the earth to man. We are to make plans, trust God, and work on those plans." In the beginning, God said, 'Let us create mankind in our image and after our likeness and let them have dominion.' However, there is one precondition. God created man in His image. Put simply, we are God's duplicates and made in His likeness. This means we are to function like God. Planning is a function of God.

Genesis 1:26 - NLT
26 *Then God said, "Let us make human beings[a] in our image, to be like us. They will reign over the fish in the sea, the birds in the sky, the livestock, all the wild animals on the earth,[b]and the small animals that scurry along the ground."*

Genesis 1:26 - NKJV

26 Then God said, "Let Us make man in Our image, according to Our likeness; let them have dominion over the fish of the sea, over the birds of the air, and over the cattle, over [a]all the earth and over every creeping thing that creeps on the earth."

Let Us and Let Them

God said, "Let *us make man and let them have dominion...."* The important part is "let us and let them". In other words, God gave the Earth to man. This is the dominion and the cultural mandate. As a result of the dominion and cultural mandate, the control of the earth is an interplay of divinity and humanity. This was a mandate that was lost in the Garden of Eden. This was the mandate that Jesus brought back and restored. Jesus said, "Go and make disciples of nations." We are to disciple nations.

Moreover, consider this Psalm of David,

Psalm 37:4-5

4 Delight yourself also in the Lord: and he shall give you the desires of your heart. 5 Commit your way unto the Lord; trust also in him, and he shall bring it to pass.

The above passage tells us that we are to delight ourselves in the Lord, commit our ways unto Him and trust in Him and He will bring our desires and plans to come to pass. So, secondly, we must understand that in addition to accepting responsibility for the earth, God wants us to entrust our plans to Him. The word "commit" means to *roll over. God wants us to roll our plans over to Him.* As we have already mentioned, as we wait on God and share our desires, God will shape them according to His plans and bring them to come to pass.

The Power of Planning

Imagine your life as a road trip across a country. Without a map or itinerary, you might miss hidden gems, take wrong turns, or waste precious time getting lost. Planning acts as your roadmap, guiding you towards your destination (your goals) and ensuring you don't waste precious time wandering aimlessly.

Planning is a Management Function

Peter F. Drucker stated that "The task of the Time Manager is to control time when he can," and according to Alan Lakein, "Control is the key concept in time management," and since planning is the key to taking control of time, then planning is a key management function.

In general, companies will rely on project managers to develop and execute plans. The objective is to ensure that projects are successfully executed. Therefore, to manage a team or several projects at the same time, you should be interested in learning how to execute an effective plan. So, how do you plan, and why is planning important in the first place? What are the key steps to executing an effective plan? What tips can help you plan your next project successfully?

Steps to Effective Planning

1. **Information Gathering**: Effective planning begins with gathering information. The more informed you are, the better your planning will be. Every purpose is established by counsel, and with good advice (information) make war. Also, in the multitude of counselors is safety and greater security (Proverbs 20: 18; 24: 6).

2. **Identify Key Resources**: Both visible and invisible resources are crucial for planning. You need tools for planning. These tools may include technology, materials, computers, boards, writing materials, recording equipment, etc.

3. **Focus on What You Have**: Avoid the mistakes that most people make. Most people focus on what they don't have. What do you currently have? What information and resources are available to you?

4. **Define Your Vision and Clarify Your Mission**: What are you truly aiming to achieve, either at a personal level or at an organizational level or even at a societal level? You need to be clear and focused. Envision your future self and define a roadmap to get there. All things are created in two dimensions: first in the mind and second in the physical. See your goal before you start planning towards it. As a man thinketh, so he is. As a man thinketh, so he becomes.

5. **Develop SMART Goals and Strategic Objectives Based on Your Plans**: SMART goals should be specific, measurable, achievable, realistic, and time-bound.

6. **Define Your Strategy:** What is the optimal way to achieve your strategic objectives? What is the global best practice? Don't settle for local achievements. What regulations must you adhere to for success? Being strategic involves considering the secondary implications of your choices and actions.

7. **Develop Frameworks and an Algorithm:** How do you plan to proceed specifically? You must break down your goals into achievable 'bite-sized' daily objectives. Tasks must be broken down into smaller tasks, and long-term goals must be broken down into intermediate goals. Intermediate goals must be broken down into short-term goals, and short-term goals must be broken down into daily tasks. What system do you intend to employ?

8. **Build Effective Teams:** Effective planning involves building teams. Team building is a skill. Effective leaders develop efficient teams, and together, teams achieve more. In other words, the sum of the parts is greater than the sum of its parts. This was one of the secrets of Benjamin Franklin.

9. **Assign Tasks:** Who are your team members? Each team member must be assigned a role. By defining the role of each team member of the team and enabling them to leverage their strengths, you enhance the

team's efficiency of the team and gain a better idea of a feasible project timeline for the project. When assigning tasks, consider each team member's availability based on their schedule and empower them to capitalize on their strengths. This is crucial and strategic for the successful implementation of plans. Also, when pairing team members, give them responsibilities that match their availability and skill set. This will enhance the overall quality of the completed project.

10. **Establish Communication Lines:** To achieve long-term strategic objectives, team members must communicate constantly. Effective communication will involve well-established communication lines. A long time ago, I learned that when a project is important, you must meet at a minimum once a week. This will ensure that deadlines are met, and important information does not fall through the cracks. There are many modern ways of communication and many tools for communication, including Zoom, video calls, emails, phone calls, in-person meetings, vision boards, etc.

11. **Tracking Progress:** You must keep track of and measure your progress. You do not have to wait for a long time to determine if you are on track. You can measure and track progress on a regular basis. You need to consider what you should be tracking and how you should track your progress. Some of the

important parameters to track include timelines, deadlines, budget, quality, and effectiveness.

12. **Evaluation:** We will need to conduct a full and final evaluation at the end of the project. This will help us in future projects and create room for improvements. The key areas to look at will depend on the nature of the project. For example, whether it was an annual conference, a building project, the launch of a new branch network, or the opening of a new franchise. In general, and as a matter of principle, key areas to consider and look at may include cost, quality, schedule, and the level of stakeholder or partner satisfaction. We need to ask, "Were you satisfied? What about your partners? What about other stakeholders? Were they satisfied?" We also need to evaluate timeliness,deadlines, etc.

Planning Tools and Techniques

A variety of tools and techniques can enhance your planning process:

1. **To-Do Lists**: Create daily or weekly to-do lists to stay organized and track your progress.

2. **Calendars:** Schedule appointments, deadlines, and important events to ensure you do not miss anything crucial.

3. **Project Management Applications:** Utilize technology to manage complex projects, set reminders, and collaborate with others.

4. **Mind Maps:** Visually brainstorm ideas, organize

thoughts, and establish connections between concepts.

Common Pitfalls of Planning and How to Avoid Them

1. **Perfectionism:** Don't let the pursuit of a perfect plan paralyze you from taking action. Start with a good-enough plan and refine it as needed.

2. **Micromanaging:** Focus on outlining the key steps without getting stuck in every minute detail. Allow for some flexibility in your plan.

3. **Unrealistic Goals:** Setting goals that are too ambitious or outside your reach can lead to discouragement. Ensure your goals are achievable within the time frame you have established.

4. **Planning Fatigue:** Taking breaks from planning is crucial to avoid burnout. Schedule time for relaxation and avoid overloading yourself.

The Law of Planning empowers you to take control of your time, navigate towards your desired future, and make the most out of your life. By incorporating the strategies and tools outlined in this chapter, you can transform your life from a series of random events into a purposeful journey of achievement. Remember, a plan is a living document, not a rigid script. Embrace the power of planning and watch your life unfold with greater clarity, focus, and success.

CHAPTER 5

LIFE PLANNING

Life is the most important journey you could ever embark on, and no one has a second chance at life. Like any expedition, the journey of life requires a well-defined plan. Life planning forms the core of this book, and this chapter lays a foundation for the rest of the book by exploring life planning inspired by two historical figures. One mastered the art of living intentionally and made significant contributions, while the other is an American psychologist who is best remembered for the hierarchy of needs, a theory in psychology that ranks human needs according to their level of importance.

Who was Benjamin Franklin?

Benjamin Franklin was one of the Founding Fathers of the United States. The Founding Fathers were known as the framers of the Constitution. He was a leading figures in colonial America who signed the Article of the Declaration of Independence and was the oldest member of the Constitutional Congress, which prepared the Constitution of the United States. Franklin was a polymath, a diplomat, and a world-renowned scientist. He founded the National Defense and was the first Postmaster General of the United States. Additionally, he was an inventor and the founder of the University of Pennsylvania. Though he did not receiving formal education, Franklin self-educated himself throughout his life through self-study and voracious reading of books.

Franklin's life illustrates the important principle that when we are young, we should learn to read, and when we are old, we should read to learn. Though self-educated, Franklin had intellectual curiosity, which stayed with him throughout his life. As an important figure in colonial America and one of the Founding Fathers, Franklin was the only one reputed to have signed all the important documents that defined and laid the foundation of colonial America. Benjamin Franklin is the figure on the one-hundred-dollar bill, even though, unlike George Washington and Thomas Jefferson, he was never President of the United States.

Lessons from Benjamin Franklin

Why was Franklin so accomplished? Why is Franklin so important in history? While in his early twenties, Franklin embarked on a personal journey to achieve moral perfection. He developed what he called his thirteen virtues. These were qualities personal to him that he thought, by achieving them in his personal life, would enable him to achieve moral perfection. His personal goal was to live without blame so he could use his creative energy to accomplish great things.

In his book *The Franklin System*, Richard Winwood writes, "In history, there are many exemplary people who achieved greatness in their lives and thereby made contributions that have benefited the world." Likewise, there are many today on similar quests. The driving force in the lives of these people has always been an ideal of some kind - a value-based idea that drove them on and kept them to the task." According to Winwood, one of the most successful people who ever lived was Benjamin Franklin, "Although of extremely humble beginnings, Franklin rose to be one of the most successful and respected men in the American colonies - a man of awesome scope and accomplishments."

Winwood further submits that to read Franklin's autobiography is to be drawn to him as he tells honestly and sweetly about his family, friends, and faults – all within "earshot" of accounts of governors, merchants, Indians, and kings. According to the autobiography of Benjamin Franklin, in 1728 Franklin ran away from his home in Boston, Massachusetts, where he was apprenticed in his elder brother's printing business, to Philadelphia, Pennsylvania. After working for various printers, he became a part owner of a printing business. In 1730, two years later, he became the sole owner of the business and began publishing *The Pennsylvania Gazette*. His name gradually became known throughout the colonies because of the success of his business. Franklin believed that in order to be successful in business, one had to simply work harder than one's competition. And Franklin did. One of his neighbors once said, "The industry of that Franklin is superior to anything that I ever saw ..." I see him still at work when I go home from the club, and he is still at work again before his neighbor Jared gets out of bed."

To quote Franklin: [7]"It was about this time I conceived the bold and arduous project of arriving at moral perfection." "I wished to live without committing any fault at any time: I would conquer all that either natural inclination, custom, or company might lead me into. As I knew or thought I knew what was right and wrong, I did not see why I might not always do the one and avoid the other." With these statements, Franklin begins the account of his most remarkable achievements and gives us a step-by-step formula to follow.

The first step Franklin took was to list and prioritize all the values (he referred to them as virtues) in his life that he wanted to perfect. Then, in order to define the action which should be associated with each value, he annexed to each a short precept that fully expressed the extent he gave to its meaning." In other words, he described for himself behavior that would be ideal within the framework of the value. These thirteen virtues formed the foundation of Franklin's life.

[8]These names of Franklin's thirteen virtues with their precepts were:

1. **TEMPERANCE.** Eat not to dullness; drink not to elevation.

---

[7] Franklin, Benjamin, The Autobiography of Benjamin Franklin and Other Writings, Penguim Classics 1986, Pg 82

[8] Franklin, Benjamin, *The Autobiography of Benjamin Franklin*, Yale University Press 1964, Pg 149 - 150.

2. **SILENCE.** Speak not but what may benefit others or yourself; avoid trifling conversation.

3. **ORDER.** Let all your things have their places; let each part of your business have its time.

4. **RESOLUTION.** Resolve to perform what you ought; perform without fail what you resolve.

5. **FRUGALITY.** Make no expense but to do good to others or yourself; i.e., waste nothing.

6. **INDUSTRY.** Lose no time; be always employed in something useful; cut off all unnecessary actions.

7. **SINCERITY.** Use no hurtful deceit; think innocently and justly, and, if you speak, speak accordingly.

8. **JUSTICE.** Wrong none by doing injuries or omitting the benefits that are your duty.

9. **MODERATION.** Avoid extremes; forbear resenting injuries as much as you think they deserve.

10. **CLEANLINESS.** Tolerate no uncleanness in body, clothes, or habitation.

11. **TRANQUILLITY.** Be not disturbed by trifles or common or unavoidable accidents.

12. **CHASTITY.** Rarely use venery except for health or offspring, never for dullness, weakness, or the injury of your own or another's peace or reputation.

13. **HUMILITY.** Imitate Jesus and Socrates.

Initially, Franklin thought he could simply refer to these virtues and their behavioral statements periodically and be sufficiently reminded of his goal. He quickly found out that such a casual approach wouldn't suffice. [9]"I soon

---

[9] Franklin, Benjamin, *The Autobiography of Benjamin Franklin and Other Writings*,

found out I had undertaken a task of more difficulty than I had imagined." While my care was employed in guarding against one fault, I was surprised by another; habit took advantage of inattention; inclination was sometimes too strong for reason."

Franklin soon realized, after some experimentation, that "daily examination would be necessary." Franklin "contrived the following method for conducting that experimentation. He made a little book in which he allotted a page for each of the virtues. He ruled each page with red ink, so as to have seven columns, one for each day, marking each column with a letter for the day. He crossed these columns with thirteen red lines, marking the beginning of each line with the first letter of one of the virtues, on which line and its proper column, I marked, by a little black spot, every fault he found upon examination to have been committed respecting that virtue on that day."

Once the "little book" was designed and completed, Franklin kept a daily account of his progress toward his goal, marking each distraction from progress by a small black spot. His ideal was to complete a day, then a week, etc., with no black spots.

As for how to acquire these virtues, Franklin advised:

Penguim Classics 1986, Pg 82

[10]"My intention was to acquire the habit of all these virtues. I judged it would be best not to distract my attention by attempting the whole at once, but to focus on one at a time; and, when I should be master of that, I would proceed to another, and so on until I should have gone through the thirteen; and, as the previous acquisition of some might facilitate the acquisition of certain others, so I arranged them with that view, as they stand above. Temperance is crucial as it tends to promote the coolness and clarity of the mind, which is so necessary where constant vigilance is to be kept up, and guarding against the persistent allure of old habits and the power of ongoing temptations." This being acquired and established, maintaining silence becomes easier; and my desire is to acquire knowledge at the same time that I improve in virtue, and considering that in conversations, knowledge is gained more by the use of the ears than of the tongue, and therefore wishing to break the habit I was getting into of prattling, and joking, which only made me appealing to superficial company. I gave Silence the second place."

Franklin was also a productivity expert. [11]Here are the 10 most important productivity lessons from Franklin's daily schedule:

---

[10] Franklin, Benjamin, The Autobiography of Benjamin Franklin and Other Writings, Penguim Classics 1986, Pg 84

[11]https://www.theladders.com/career-advice/lessons-from-benjamin-franklins-daily-schedule-that-will-double-your-productivity, May 30, 2019

1. Keep it simple

The first thing to note about Franklin's daily schedule is its simplicity. There are only six time blocks allocated each day, and one of these blocks includes sleep—an obvious necessity. There's no overwhelming to-do list of things to get done. It's simple, focused on essentials, and highly effective. It's easy to underestimate the power of simplicity, even though it's the hidden driving force behind peak productivity.

2. Go to bed and wake up at the same time each day

One of Franklin's most popular mantras was "early to bed and early to rise makes a man healthy, wealthy, and wise," and according to this schedule, he definitely lived up to it. Each day, Franklin woke up early at 5am and went to bed early at 10 pm, for a total of 7 hours of sleep each night. It's important to note, however, that what matters most isn't the time you go to bed or wake up, it's the consistency of your sleep schedule. By going to bed and waking up at the same time each day, you'll train your brain to fall asleep faster and improve the quality of your sleep.

3. Spend quiet time alone

Shortly after waking up, Franklin would take a shower and then "address Powerful Goodness." In other words, he'd spend some time in prayer or meditation. This daily habit of solitude gave Franklin the much needed clarity and focus to plan the day, and follow through on his plans.

4. Set your intention and plan for the day

Each morning, before going to work, Franklin would set his intention for the day with an important question: What good shall I do this day? Then he'd pick a virtue to focus on and begin to "contrive day's business and take the resolution of the day i.e To plan his day." Setting an intention and creating a plan of action each morning ensures that you stay focused on your most important task and avoid getting easily distracted by the minutiae and other people during the day.

5. Dedicate time to learning

In Franklin's daily schedule, he sets aside some time to "prosecute the present study," which means he would spend time on an independent personal project separate from work. Most likely, this would have been time spent reading either books or papers. Alternatively, you could spend this time learning a language, playing an instrument, or on your hobbies.

6. Create time blocks for deep and shallow work

To plan his day, Franklin created time blocks to manage his time effectively and protect his day from unexpected interruptions. Specifically, Franklin allocated two four-hour time blocks—from 8am till 12 pm, and from 2pm till 6 pm—for deep work and uninterrupted focus on his most important tasks. Likewise, Franklin allocated a two-hour time block—from 12 pm till 2 pm— for lunch and shallow work, i.e., reviewing his finances. By creating time blocks in this manner, Franklin finished his most important tasks for the day when he had the most energy to do so.

7. Put things back in order after work

After a long tiring day at work, it's easy to walk away from our workspace and leave things in a disorderly manner, only to return the next morning to clean it up before getting back to work. Even though this saves time upfront, it wastes valuable time, willpower, and energy that could have been spent working on important tasks straight away. To avoid this problem, Franklin made sure to clean up his workspace and put things back in order before leaving the office each day. This ensured that Franklin had enough willpower each morning to tackle the tedious tasks in the long day ahead.

8. Schedule downtime

After work each day, Franklin would clean up his workspace, eat dinner, and spend the rest of the evening relaxing: listening to music and catching up with his friends. Downtime isn't a waste of time. It's a powerful productivity tool for re-energizing the brain and body in preparation for the challenges of the next day.

9. Reflect on your day in the evening

Just before going to bed, Franklin would reflect on his day and ask himself an important question: What good have I done today? After noting what went well and what didn't go so well during the day, Franklin would look to change and improve his daily schedule. Similarly, an evening audit of your daily productivity will help you uncover time-wasting activities that drain your energy and improve your daily schedule for better productivity.

10. Don't aim for perfection

In the book "*Daily Rituals: How Artists Work (Audiobook)*", Currey explains that Franklin himself struggled to stick to his daily schedule: "He was not naturally inclined to keep his papers and other possessions organized, and he found the effort so vexing that he almost quit in frustration. Moreover, the demands of his printing business meant that he couldn't always follow the exact daily timetable that he set for himself." What matters most isn't perfectionism; it's improvement, as Franklin emphasized.

Who Was Abraham Maslow?

Abraham Harold Maslow [12]was born on April 1st 1908 to first-generation Jewish immigrants from Kiev, Ukraine and died on June 8th 1970. Maslow attended the City College of New York after high school. In 1926 he began taking legal studies classes at night in addition to his undergraduate course load. He hated it and almost immediately dropped out. In 1927 he transferred to Cornell, but he left after just one semester due to poor grades and high costs. He later graduated from City College and went to graduate school at the University of Wisconsin to study psychology. In 1928, he married his first cousin Bertha, who was still in high school at the time. The pair had met in Brooklyn years earlier. A *Review of General Psychology* survey, published in 2002, ranked Maslow as the tenth most cited psychologist of the 20th century. Maslow was a psychology professor at Brandeis University, Brooklyn College, New School for Social Research, and Columbia University.

Maslow's Hierarchy of Need

As an American psychologist, Abraham Maslow is best known for his hierarchy of needs, which is a theory in psychology that ranks human needs in order of importance. It is a psychological health predicated on fulfilling innate human needs in priority and culminating in self-actualization. Maslow stressed the importance of focusing on

---

[12] https://en.wikipedia.org/wiki/Abraham_Maslow, last edited on October 31st, 2024 by 4:14 (UTC)

the positive qualities in people, as opposed to treating them as a bag of symptoms.

What is a Pyramid of Productivity?

A Pyramid of Productivity, according to Biology Online [13]is a graphical representation in the shape of a pyramid showing the distribution of productivity or flow of energy through the trophic levels. In the Pyramid of Productivity, the lower trophic levels have more energy than the higher trophic levels. Hence, the bottom level has the greatest energy, whereas the top has the lowest. Therefore, the diagram resembles a pyramid to show that for the ecosystem to sustain itself, there must be more energy at lower trophic levels to maintain a stable population. The synonym of Pyramid of Productivity is Productivity Pyramid.

Winwood's Productivity Pyramid

According to Richard Winwood:

[14]"Some years ago, after researching a paper I was writing about human motivation, I reviewed the works of Abraham Maslow, particularly his famous 'Hierarchy of Needs.' It occurred to me that if I were to overlay Mallow's pyramid with the basic elements of goal achievement, using values as a base, I would have a simple model of values-based goal achievement".".

---

[13] https://www.biologyonline.com/dictionary/pyramid-of-productivity, last updated on February 24th, 2022

[14] *Winwood, Richard I., Time Management: An Introduction to The Franklin System, Franklin International Institute 1990, Pg 36*

"The idea was put on the back burner for several years. I did use it on several occasions, primarily to show subordinates how values-based goal setting worked. Then, one day, I was invited to attend a time management seminar taught by a friend. My friend, as part of the seminar, was trying to show the continuity between values and goal setting. "Wow," I thought. "I've got a model that shows that relationship!" After some tinkering with the model, the *Winwood* Productivity Pyramid was "born."

The Productivity Pyramid is a model of life planning that illustrates the relationship and continuity between values and goal setting. It is a values-based method. This model is why Benjamin Franklin was both effective and the most accomplished man in American history. It is a tool for life planning. Anyone who can spare 10 - 15 minutes to plan their day and who is equipped with the right model and planning tools will become a very effective individual.

Habits that support your Life Plan:
1. Start Small: Don't overwhelm yourself. Begin with a small, achievable habit and gradually increase the difficulty as it becomes ingrained in your routine.
2. Focus on Consistency: The key to forming habits is consistency. Strive to practice your desired habit daily, even if it is for a short duration."
3. Track Your Progress: Seeing your progress is a powerful motivator. Use habit trackers or journals to monitor your consistency and celebrate milestones.

4. Reward Yourself: Positive reinforcement strengthens habits. Reward yourself for sticking to your plan and achieving milestones.

Benjamin Franklin's life offers valuable lessons for life planning. One of his most famous tools is his daily schedule, meticulously crafted to maximize his productivity. He divided his day into specific blocks dedicated to different tasks, ensuring he focused on what mattered most.

Another key concept from Benjamin Franklin is the idea of virtues." He identified 13 virtues he aimed to cultivate throughout his life, such as temperance, order, and resolution. By working on these virtues, he actively shaped his character and directed his life towards personal excellence. Also, Abraham Maslow's Hierarchy of Need provided a framework for life planning. This pyramid-shaped model proposes that human needs are arranged in a hierarchy, with basic physiological needs like food and shelter forming the foundation. As these basic needs are met, we strive to fulfill higher-level needs such as love and belonging, esteem, and ultimately, self-actualization – reaching our full potential.

The principles of life planning outlined in this chapter can transform your life from a series of random events into a purposeful journey towards a life of fulfillment.

Challenge

Creating Your Personalized Life Plan

1. Take time to identify Your Core Values: What truly matters to you in life? Take time for introspection to identify your core values. Go on a journey of self-discovery and God-discovery.

2. Develop a Daily Schedule and adhere to it: Develop a daily schedule that prioritizes high-impact tasks, incorporates essential activities, and allows for flexibility.

3. Set SMART Goals and follow them: Establish long-term, mid-term, and short-term goals using the SMART framework (Specific, Measurable, Achievable, Relevant, and Time-bound).

4. Learn to Build Systems: Identify key habits that support your goals and create a plan. Turn the plan into systems for consistent implementation.

5. Sharpen the Saw by scheduling Regular Reviews: Block time in your calendar for regular reviews of your life plan. This will help you to track progress and make necessary adjustments where needed.

CHAPTER 6

THE REALITY AND LIFE TEST

Introduction

In this chapter, we are dealing with the Reality and Life Check. Before we embark on the planning process, you will need to take the Reality and Life Test. What is a Reality and Life Test? These are a set of questions that have been specially prepared to help you kick-start the planning process. A Reality and Life Test is like your vitals, which are usually required when you visit the doctor's office. Your vital signs tell us the state of your health. A Reality and Life Test when properly completed should tell us the state of your life. In this book, we are dealing with life planning. The focus of life planning is on your long-term priorities that will ensure that you fulfill the ultimate agenda for your life. Planning is a process. There are many models and frameworks for planning. In this book, we are using the Franklin system. In the Reality and Life Test, we are dealing with three sets of questions: where are you now, where are you going, and how would you get there? When planning looks into the future, it is referred to as a strategic plan.

About Alfred Nobel

[15]The Nobel Prizes may be one of the most famous and prestigious awards in the world – but who was the man

---

[15] https://theconversation.com/the-extraordinary-life-of-alfred-nobel, published on Oct 11, 2024, by 8:04 am

behind them? Alfred Bernhardt Nobel was a Swedish chemist, inventor, engineer, entrepreneur, and businessman. He also wrote poetry and drama. Alfred Nobel born on October 21st, 1833, and he died on December 10th, 1896. According to Ingrid Carlberg's biography of Nobel, he had a tough childhood in Stockholm. Not only was he poor, but the boy who would become an esteemed scientist – holding 355 patents in his lifetime – was placed in a class for children with learning difficulties at school. Innovation may have run in the Nobel blood; however, Alfred's father, Immanuel, was also an inventor, albeit less successful than his son would become." Mr. Nobel is best remembered for the invention of dynamite, which was patented in 1867.

Alfred Nobel Wrote His Own Obituary

[16]In 1888 Nobel was astonished to read his own obituary, titled "The Merchant of Death Is Dead", in a French newspaper. However, it was Alfred's brother Ludvig who had died. The mistaken announcement of Alfred Nobel's death was eight years premature. The article had a profound impact on Nobel and made him reconsider his legacy and how he would like to be remembered. The above story challenged and inspired Nobel to redo his will. On December 10th, 1896, Alfred Nobel died in his villa in San Remo, Italy, from a cerebral hemorrhthe agege at age 63 years. [17]In his last will, Nobel specified that his fortune be used to create a

---

[16] https://en.wikipedia.org/wiki/Nobel_Prize#:, Page last updated on October 22, 2024 by 6:54 am (UTC)

[17] https://www.britannica.com/topic/Nobels-will, Oct. 12, 2024, 9:52 AM ET (AP)

series of prizes for those who confer the "greatest benefit on mankind" in the areas of physics, chemistry, physiology or medicine, literature, and peace. [18]Nobel bequeathed 94% of his total assets, 31 million SEK (approximately US$186 million, €150 million in 2008), to establish the five Nobel Prizes. As a result of skepticism surrounding the will,, it was not approved until April 26th, 1897. Ragnar Sohlman and Rudolf Liljenquist, the Executors of the will formed the Nobel Foundation to take care of the fortune and to organize the awarding of prizes.

Lessons from Alfred Nobel

How would you like to be remembered when you pass on from this world? What will be your legacy? Will you finish your race? Will you reach your highest potential? Will you fulfill and finish your purpose? As a result of a mistaken obituary announcement, about which historians do not even agree, Alfred Nobel rewrote his own obituary, in that way, influenced and predicting how he would be remembered by future generations. But first, he had to invest his life in amassing enough wealth to fund his dream and to leave his footprints indelibly on the sands of time.

Lessons from Paul the Apostle

In the introduction to my book, *"Striving for Mastery: Lessons from the Life of Paul"*, I wrote, "Who is Paul the apostle and why should we have another book based on his life? Have you ever wondered how Paul the apostle would

---

[18] https://en.wikipedia.org/wiki/Nobel_Prize#:, Page last updated on October 22, 2024 by 6:54 am (UTC)

have lived if he were born in the 20th century and alive in the 21st century? Who was Paul? How did he live? What kind of Christian was Paul? Why another book on the principles on which his life was based?" How did Paul's letters make it into Scripture and become permanent documents that have been read and re-read for centuries? Those were some of the questions that captured my thoughts as a young believer."

At the end of his life, Paul wrote his valedictory speech:

2 Timothy 4: 6-8 - NKJV
6 For I am already being poured out as a drink offering, and the time of my departure is at hand. 7 I have fought the good fight, I have finished the race, I have kept the faith. 8 Finally, there is laid up for me the crown of righteousness, which the Lord, the righteous Judge, will give to me on that Day, and not only to me but also to all who have loved His appearing.

[19]"Paul is one of the few people in history who, as he approached the end, looked into the world beyond with a degree of expectancy of his eternal reward." I am sure there would have been many unanswered questions on his mind, but he did not look towards the end with his heart in trepidation. In his own words, he said, "For I am now ready to be offered, and the time of my departure is at hand."

---

[19] Enelamah, John C., Striving for the Mastery: Lessons from the Life of Paul, JEM Publishing 2016, Pg 10-11

The phrase "I am now ready to be offered" in the King James Version is rendered as "I am ready being poured out as a drink offering" in the New Kings James Version and the New International Version. The apostle lived a life of service to humanity. He allowed his life to be poured out, emptying himself of the gifts and talents he was born with. He used his earthly resources to serve his generation. We will read from this book that Paul the apostle was a servant, a pioneer, and a builder of men and of local churches.

He was referring to his impending death when he talked about his departure. This implied that he had answered some of the fundamental questions about this present life. For example, what is life on earth about? Why all the labor to become and to have? What do you look forward to as you approach the end? What is a man's reward for his earthly labor? "

That statement also enables us to understand why Paul might have won many of his personal battles in life. He described his exit from this world as a departure; he was taking a trip into eternity. I believe this statement gives us further insight into the mindset of the apostle. It empowers us to understand how his mind was working and why Paul was a driven person – mono-focused.

The apostle was conscious of this present world and mindful of the world to come. He was leaving this present world and taking a trip to the world beyond. When you travel, you have to plan both your departure and your arrival. You need a mental picture not just of your present location but of your arrival location. Your understanding of where you are going will influence how you plan and pack for your trip.

The ability to do this with life itself is a sign of true greatness, and it can be emulated and learned. Paul's mindset enabled him to hold the things of this world lightly. Paul worked hard to become, in order to serve, rather than primarily to have. For example, Paul as an apostle could have relied on others early in his ministry for his upkeep, but rather he made tents to pay for his calling. He later explains that his primary reason for doing this was to leave no one in doubt of his primary reason for being in ministry."

Paul is an example of a man who strove for mastery and ran his race to a conclusion. Like Jesus, Paul left the example of the process and prize of an effective and successful life. I define success as running in your lane, fulfilling your high calling from God and finishing your particular race. Take a moment and find out where you are to understand what it will take to go to where you are meant to be by taking a life check.

Take The Reality and Life Test:

1. Surname ____

2. Given name____

3. Sex ______________ 4. Date of Birth __________________

5. Age _________ 6. Are you happy? ____________________

7. Are you fulfilled? ________________________________

8. Are you content with your life? ____________________

9. How much longer do you think you will live?

____

10. What do you do with your time?

____

11. Can you account for the last week of your life?

____

12. Do you have any products in the market? ____________

13. How many inventions or books are to your name?

____

____

14. How would you like to be remembered?

____

____

15. Do you believe in a life mission?

____

16. Do you know your life mission?

____

17. If not, what will you do about it?

____

18. Make finding your life mission your mission in life.
What steps will you take to accomplish this?

____

19. On a scale of 1 - 10, 1 being the least and 10 being the most,
where are you in terms of fulfilling your life mission?

____

20. What is your greatest heart desire?

____

21. What do you want most out of this life?

____

22. The Apple company has versions of their products, why?

____

23. When will you become the best version of yourself?

____

____

24. What do you consider to be the greatest impediment to becoming the best version of yourself?

____

____

25. How many forms of education exist _______________

26. How educated are you? _______________________

27. Do you have a personal library? ________________

28. How many books do you have? ________________

29. How often do you read? ______________________

30. How many books do you read in a year? _________

31. Whom do you admire the most and why?

____

32. Why do you admire this person?

____

33. Have you ever failed in life?

____

36. How and where did you fail?

____

____

37. What lessons did you take away?

____

38. In a few words, write your own obituary (use additional material if needed).

____

____

____

____

____

____

____

____

____

____

____

____

____

____

CHAPTER 7

THE FRANKLIN SYSTEM
OF TIME MANAGEMENT

This chapter equips you with practical tools for life planning. It introduces the Franklin System of Time Management, also known as the Franklin System. The Franklin system emphasizes values, purposeful living, planning, goal setting, and daily routines. We will also review the concept of a Productivity Pyramid, which will help us understand Benjamin Franklin's Time Management System of Life Planning.

Understanding the Productivity Pyramid

What is a major lesson from the Life of Benjamin Franklin? It is the fact that Benjamin Franklin accomplished so much in one lifetime. Judging from his achievements, it is as if Benjamin Franklin lived multiple lifetimes in one lifetime. Franklin experienced the multiplication of days and the addition of years of life.

Proverbs 9:10-11

[10] The fear of the Lord is the beginning of wisdom: and the knowledge of the holy is understanding. [11] For by me thy days shall be multiplied, and the years of thy life shall be increased.

In Proverbs 9: 10, the phrase "For by me thy days shall be multiplied" means productive days, and the phrase "and the years of thy life shall be increased" means years of life will be added to you, resulting in a long life. When you combine these two phrases, Proverbs 9:11 states that if we fear God and avoid evil, we will live a long life full of productive days, with each day looking longer than 24 hours as a result of our productivity level and the actual results from our lives. Franklin understood the concept of time and planning, and through planning lived his life in a way that he touched his life purpose every day. We can also do the same. Planning is a fundamental law of the universe and can simply be defined as predetermining the future. Planning is a primary tool for taking control of our lives. We control our lives by controlling how we spend our time. In addition to understanding time and planning, another major reason Benjamin Franklin was so productive and accomplished was because of his "little book."

The Struggle to Plan the Future

Every new calendar year, millions of people attempt to start the year by making New Year's resolutions. Unfortunately, very few get far with their resolutions. By the third week of January most would have gone back to their daily routines, if they get that far. Why do many people fail to achieve lasting success with New Year resolutions? Why do many New Year resolutions not work? There are a number of reasons why New Year resolutions do not work and why many fail to achieve lasting success with them.

Starting life planning with your day instead of ending with your day puts the cart before the horse. Practicing life planning while making New Year resolutions is like traveling into your future with a cart-drawn horse. You will not go far, if you go at all. Secondly, it is very difficult, if not nearly impossible, to live your life in a manner that is inconsistent with your basic beliefs. Our actions are a product of our belief system. It is easy to resolve on January 1st, 2025, that you will stop smoking and kick the habit. However, you are not likely to stop smoking if you love to smoke. Therefore, the resolution to stop smoking will not last long unless you develop a hatred for smoking or replace the habit of smoking with a superior habit.

Most materials and teachings on goal setting and life planning focus too heavily on daily activities. They often start with the day. As a result of his devotion to finding methods and techniques for maximizing his life and getting a lot done in a short time, Franklin kept self-educating himself until he became one of the most educated men in the colonies. Though Franklin divided his day into six blocks and found a way to be productive throughout the day, Franklin's Time Management System ended with his daily tasks. It did not start with his daily tasks. This is a major difference and a dramatic departure from many of the existing goal-setting and life planning formulas out there. Franklin's formula for life planning is contrarian.

According to Franklin, he continued to refine his methods

and techniques throughout his life. However, as he contrived each day's activities, he always began his day with the morning question, "What good shall I do today?" and ended each day with the evening question, "What good have I done today?" Under the virtue of Order, he expanded this idea to include a daily planning regimen where he formulated his daily tasks (which always included personal study) and made a daily resolution. His "little book" was used as a guide for both remembering his commitments and also to track his progress."[20]

Writing in his autobiography at the age of seventy-nine, Franklin records:

"I entered upon the execution of this plan for self-examination and continued it, with occasional intermissions for some time . . . .but I always carried my little book with me... . . . And it may well be that my posterity should be informed of this little artifice (his little book) with the blessing of God, their ancestor owed the constant felicity of his life down to his 79th year on which this is written. I hope, therefore, that some of my descendants may follow the example and reap the benefit."[21]

Franklin's "little Book" ensured that he followed a system of time management that came to be described as the "Benjamin Franklin Time Management System."

---

[20] *Winwood, Richard I., Time Management: An Introduction to The Franklin System, Franklin International Institute 1990, Pg 44*

[21] Winwood, Richard I., *Time Management: An Introduction to The Franklin System, Franklin International Institute 1990, Pg 45*

Benjamin Franklin's System of Time Management and Life Planning

Franklin understood the concept of time. Most quotes we have about time came from Franklin. It was Franklin who taught us that "Time is Money." One of Franklin's quotes states:

"Dost thou love life? Then do not squander time; for that's the stuff life is made of."

Introducing the Franklin System

The Franklin System is a time management approach inspired by Benjamin Franklin's meticulous planning habits and thirteen virtues. Franklin is remembered for so many things and was very accomplished. However, the Franklin System of Time Management is one of Franklin's greatest discoveries and gifts to the world. It is a systematic approach to life. The Franklin System of Time Management is a Productivity Pyramid, a monolith with six blocks, which are also levels. The Franklin System is not only a formula but a concept on how to organize your life around your goals. The Franklin system is made up of six levels. Each level builds on the previous one. This is the direct application of the law of compounding. As already explained, the law of compounding states that life on Earth compounds. This is true of the Franklin system. It is a formula for planning and achieving success in this life by fulfilling your God-ordained purpose.

We will take the next several chapters to explain the concept and formula, and then we will end up with a case study.

What is a Formula?

A formula is a mathematical relationship or rule expressed in symbols. A formula is also a list of ingredients with which something is made. A formula is a general fact, rule, or principle expressed in usually mathematical symbols. A formula can also be described as a system for achieving a predetermined result. Benjamin Franklin Productivity Pyramid is a formula for life planning and for making success out of this life. It is made up of six composite parts that are interdependent.

Models of the Franklin System:

The Winwood Model

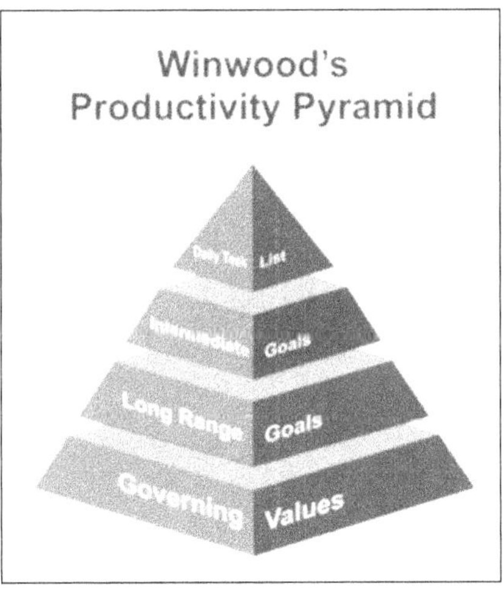

Figure 1.0

The Winwood Productivity Pyramid, a model of the Franklin system depicted in Figure 1.0, consists of four levels. According to Winwood, [22]"The model has at its base the highest priorities of our personal lives or of our organization -Governing Values. When identified and expanded upon, these values provide the rules or principles guiding the goal-setting process." Long-range goals are then set within the framework of the Governing Values. Intermediate goals are formulated based on the long-range goals. Finally, the process culminates in a list of "daily tasks" or personal daily behaviour."

The Winwood model consists of four levels and blocks:

1. Level 1 - Governing Values
2. Level 2 - Long Range Goals
3. Level 3 - Intermediate Goals
4. Level 4 - Daily Task List

---

[22] Winwood, Richard I, *Time Management: An Introduction to the Franklin System,* Franklin International Institute Inc., 1990 pg 37-38

The Adelaja Model

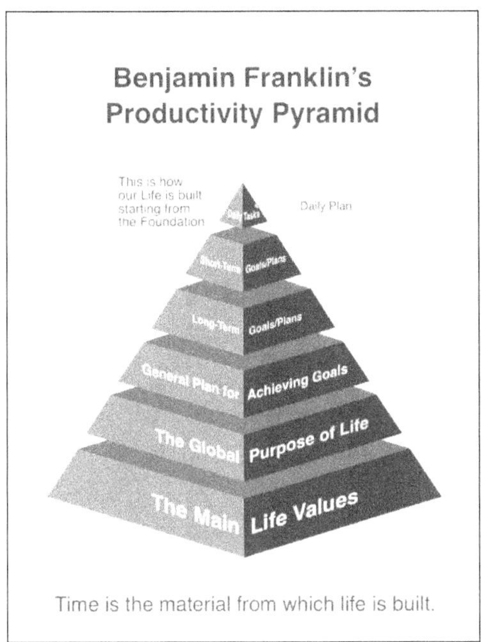

Figure 1.1

However, this book is based on a slightly modified model made popular by Dr. Sunday Adelaja. Adelaja surmised that "Benjamin Franklin was faced with an acute shortage of time and then Franklin invented the Franklin Time Management system that allowed him to act several times more efficiently than an ordinary person. According to Adelaja, the Time Management system taught at many time management courses, is 'directed backwards' - they are based on the accounting of the already used, worked time, it is a kind of diary of what has been done." Whereas "the Franklin system is directed forward - it works with what needs to be done." The Adelaja model consists of six floors instead of four as in the Winwood model. Adelaja introduces two new levels not in the Winwood model called Global Life Purpose and

95

General Plan for Achieving Purpose. He also uses the terminology Long-term goals instead of long-range goals and mid-term goals instead of intermediate goals. Also, in the Adelaja model, the long-term and mid-term goals are on the same level and floor, while he introduces short-term goals as a fifth floor.

According to Adelaja, the Franklin System is a monolith with six levels or six floors. The Franklin system is a major key, an Almighty Formula for life planning, and is at the core of this book. It emphasizes values, purpose, planning, goal setting, and ends with a daily plan to ensure your actions align with your long-term vision in a way that you touch your purpose every day.

Key Blocks and Levels of the Adelaja Model of the Franklin System:

We will highlight and describe each level of the Adelaja model, explaining their meanings and the interconnectivity between all the levels. In the rest of this book, anytime we use the term "the Franklin system," we are referring to the Adelaja model depicted in Figure 1.1.

1. Level 1 - The Main Life Values (calling, dream, motivation, and mission).
2. Level 2 - Global Life Purpose (vision).
3. Level 3 - General Plan for Achieving Success (methods and tools).
4. Level 4 - Long-term Plan (long-term goals 20-25 years and intermediate goals 5-10 years).

5. Level 5 - Short-term Plan (short-term goal 1 year or less).

6. Level 6 - Daily Task (plan for the day - schedules, habits, routines, and to-do lists).

CHAPTER 8

THE MAIN LIFE VALUES

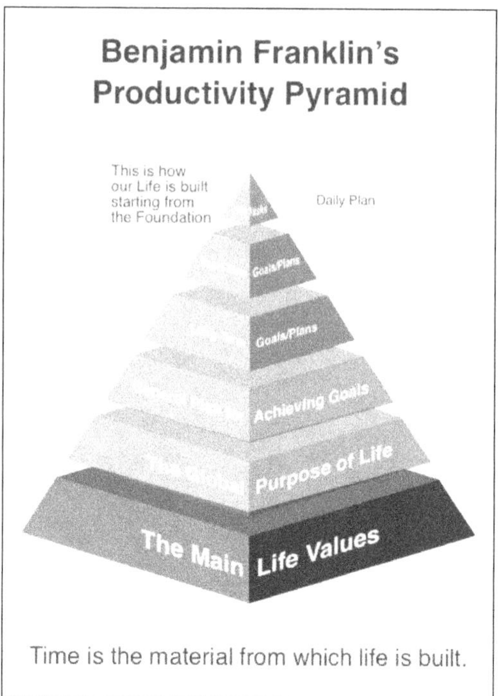

Figure 1.2

At this level of The Main Life Values, we answer the questions of calling, passion, mission, values, motivation, and our highest priorities for living. The Franklin System of Time Management, though shaped like a pyramid, is akin to a high-rise building with six floors. What are governing values? [23]"Governing values are simply a description of one's

---

[23] Smith, Hyrum W., The Three Gaps: Are You Making A Difference, Berrett-Koehler, Inc. 2015, pg. 36

highest priorities." Your governing life values form the main values of your life. In his book, *The 10 Natural Laws of Successful Time and Life Management*, Hyrum Smith states the Second Law as [24]"Your governing values are the foundation of personal fulfillment." Smith is correct. You cannot achieve lasting success unless your life is founded on the right values. Therefore, the main values represent your governing principles and form the substantial base and foundation of the entire structure of the Franklin system. It serves as the support for all other levels and upholds the rest of the structure. In his book *System Building: The Key to Resolving Every Problem and Attaining Every Goal*, Sunday Adelaja states, "Personally, I believe the main values of life should be connected to heaven." I agree with Adelaja for several reasons. Firstly, we all originated from heaven and are merely stewards of what we have received in this life. Secondly, Jesus set an example that we should follow in His footsteps. Jesus mentioned that His nourishment was to carry out the will of the Father and complete His work (John 4: 34). Thirdly, our ultimate purpose in life is to please God who dwells in heaven, and what better place to get our marching orders than from being connected with Him.

The Franklin System of Time Management is a Productivity Pyramid, which serves as a model for life planning that illustrates the connection and continuity between values and

---

[24] Smith, Hyrum W., *The 10 Natural Laws of Successful Time and Life Management: Proven Strategies for Increased Productivity and Inner Peace*, Warner Books, A Time Warner Company 1994, pg. 46

goal setting. The Franklin System is a values-based goal achievement method. Level one of the Franklin System is constructed on the solid foundation of Values which provide support for all the other levels. This strong base of Values is the primary reason why most New Year's resolutions fail to materialize. They are not rooted in values and, as a result, are not value-based. Since no one can perform consistently in a manner that is at variance with their core values, most New Year's resolutions are destined to fail. New Year's resolutions violate the fundamental law of change, which is first within, and then without.

What do values entail? Values represent our highest priorities in this life. Your values not only represent your highest priorities, but they also reveal a lot about your calling, mission, passion, and dreams buried in the innermost chambers of your life. Usually in this life, when you are unsure what God has called you to, you have to consider the people, the places, and the things you admire, especially the people, and start to ask, why? For example, my brother, Dr. Okechukwu Enelamah from the very first time he heard about Harvard Business School (HBS), was fascinated by HBS. Why? HBS formed an integral and important part of his eternal destiny. There was something waiting for him in Boston, that perhaps he was not going to get in any other place. Your values represent the things that propel you to your highest calling. They are core, foundational, and central.

Jesus said His food was to do the will of His Father and to finish His work. Therefore, **The Main Values of Life deal** with our calling, mission, values, and motivation. We were created by God to fulfill a specific purpose and assignment. This should be the driving force of our lives and our basic motivation. We are to live according to the counsel of God's will. Like Jesus we are to be obsessed with doing the will of God. Jesus' statement in John 4: 34 should also be our statement of purpose and passion.

John 4:33-34

33 Therefore said the disciples one to another, "Has any man brought him anything to eat?" 34 Jesus said unto them, "My food is to do the will of him who sent me and to finish his work." " "

Like Jesus, we are to be consumed by the will of God. Our prayer should be "Thy kingdom come; thy will be done on earth." We are to be obsessed with doing God's will and seeing His kingdom established. The reason we live is to do the will of God. We are here on Earth to please God. Our commitment is to God and to be used by Him to do His bidding. The reason we wake up every day should be to please God. Any other obsession or commitment will lead to self-destruction. For Benjamin Franklin, his thirteen virtues, which were truly the driving force of his life, became the cornerstone on which his life was built. So, at the foundation of the Franklin System of Time Management are your Governing Life Values or The Main Values for Living. The thirteen virtues served as a personal constitution. Values not only represent our highest priorities, but they also are the reasons we live and help shape the boundaries of our lives. Values give us a purpose to wake up every day.

The process of determining our personal values is described as valuing or a valuation process. According to Winwood, "Valuing is a process of crystallizing your highest priorities into a set of value statements." These value statements then form the basis for discovering your purpose, planning your life, and setting goals, implying a system of values. You must have a reason why a goal is important to you. Goals will vary from person to person depending on their priorities, which essentially reflect their value system. We will prioritize life according to our values.

At the bottom of the Franklin System of Time Management are your governing life values, the reasons you do what you do. Unless you clarify your values, it will be more difficult to determine or discover your purpose. Why do you get up every day? What drives you? What is your greatest heart's desire? All the above questions touch on your values.

What Are Your Values?
A major part of life planning is settling down to clarify your values. According to the late Dick Kramer of Nigerian Arthur Andersen, Andersen Consulting and African Capital Alliance there are three sets of questions you need to ask yourself at every point in time: where am I? Where do I want to go, and

how do I get there? In planning, you will need a quiet place and writing materials. All planning is abstract until goals or plans are written down. Once we write things down, they transition from abstract to concrete.

Discovering Your Governing Life Values

Now that you understand the significance of governing life values in the Franklin System, it's time to embark on a journey of self-discovery and God-discovery. In identifying your personal values, you must remember it is a personal journey. Wherever you land and whatever you decide or find will be personal to you. You are attempting to identify your unique voice and the unique person that you are. Those who compare themselves or compete with others are not wise.

Here are some exercises to help you identify your core values:

1. Self-evaluation of Priorities: [25]According to Winwood, "using Benjamin Franklin's method, begin to evaluate the highest priorities of your life, your personal values. What are the most important things to you? If you 'boil out' all the relative trivialities of your life and get down to the bedrock of your existence, what do you find? This is obviously a personal, introspective process -- you are looking inward at yourself."

2. Life Role Exploration: Consider the various roles you play in life (e.g., spouse, parent, friend, professional).

---

[25] Winwood, Richard I, *Time Management: An Introduction to the Franklin System,* Franklin International Institute, Inc. 1990, pg. 45

What qualities do you strive to embody in each role? What principles guide your behavior within these roles?

3. Self-reflection on Values: Reflect on past decisions you have made. What values were most evident in those choices? What motivated you? Conversely, are there past decisions that clashed with your true values? What can you learn from these experiences?

4. Looking into the Future: Imagine your life ten years from now, living to your fullest potential. What aspects of your life bring you the most joy and fulfillment? What principles guided you on this path?

The Power of a Personal Constitution

Values are deeply held beliefs, and valuing, according to Hyrum Smith, "is the process of crystallizing our highest priorities into a set of value statements." Why do you do what you do? What is your greatest heart's desire? What do you want most in this life? If you were to answer these questions, it would lead to a Personal Constitution, that will help you develop your Personal Mission statement.

What is a Personal Constitution?

A Personal Constitution is a guiding document that outlines who you are and what your highest priorities are. It articulates how you would like to live your life daily, and when followed, will allow you to reach your long-range, long-term goals, ultimately attaining your highest desires and fulfilling your potential. You should be able to develop your Personal Mission statement from your Personal

Constitution. In his book *How to Create Your Own Dynamic Mission Statement that Works*, Peter J. Daniels, an international Christian businessman from Australia and the founder of World Centre for Entrepreneurial Studies wrote, "I have been involved in business for over 35 years, coming into contact with people from all walks of life in many countries of the world. I have observed that most serious, thoughtful people have a mission statement of some kind."

Hyrum Smith believes that "your governing values are the foundation of personal fulfillment," and I agree. In order to achieve lasting success, you must be at peace with your inner self. The reason most New Year resolutions do not work is simply because it is impossible to consistently perform in a manner that is inconsistent with your core values, fundamental makeup, or belief system. Your core values will touch the deepest part of your essence because the purpose for which you were created is encoded in your DNA.

You were brought into this world for a specific reason, and that purpose not only shapes your values but it is also the driving force of your life. It is impossible to live a life of significance without being inwardly motivated. Jesus stated, "My food is to do the will of Him who sent me, and to finish His work." The reason Jesus lived to fulfill God's will and complete the assignment committed into His hands. He lived with a purpose within a purpose, and that was the driving force of His existence. This is why He got up a great while before the day and prayed (Mark 1:35). Why do you live? What drives you? Why do you get up every day? You will need to answer these questions to make the most of your life. Your Personal Constitution and your Personal Mission statement will help you make the most of your life.

Benjamin Franklin developed his Thirteen virtues, which were his personal constitution, and they shaped the rest of his life. He attributed all he accomplished to striving to live by these thirteen virtues. Those virtues, which were his main values for living, shaped his life and guided him to becoming one of the most accomplished Americans and the most famous of the Founding Fathers also known as the Framers of the American Constitution. By adhering to these values, Franklin lived multiple lifetimes in one lifetime. Your values not only tell us who you are, they are who you are. Since your values form the foundation of your personal fulfillment, lasting success comes from living a life aligned with your core values, which leads to inner peace.

Crafting Your Personal Constitution

Inspired by Benjamin Franklin's thirteen virtues, create your own personal constitution – a written declaration of your core values and guiding principles. This document serves as a constant reminder of what truly matters to you.

Crafting Your Personal Constitution Template:

1. **My Core Values:** List 5-10 values that are most important to you (e.g., integrity, growth, family, adventure).
2. **Guiding Principles:** For each core value, define specific principles that translate that value into action. For example,

for the core value of "integrity," a guiding principle might be "honesty in all my dealings."

3. **Life Goals:** How will your core values and principles guide your life goals? Briefly outline your long-term aspirations in various areas of your life (e.g., career, relationships, personal growth).

Defining Family and Corporate Values

The concept of a Personal Constitution can be extended to families and corporations. Establishing a set of shared values creates a foundation for decision-making, fostering a unified and purposeful environment.

Steps to integrating your values into your life plan:

1. **Identifying Your Core Values:** What truly matters to you? Is it family, adventure, financial security, creativity, or making a positive impact on the world? Reflect on what makes your life feel meaningful.

2. **Value-Based Decision Making:** When faced with choices, ask yourself if the decision aligns with your core values. This ensures your life plan reflects your deepest desires and guides you towards a fulfilling path.

3. **Creating a Value Statement:** Craft a concise statement that encapsulates your core values. This statement can serve as a guiding principle for your life plan and decision-making.

Conclusion

The Franklin System of Life Planning is not a rigid set of

rules, but a flexible framework. It empowers you to take control of your time and to translate the philosophy of life planning into actionable steps. By incorporating the Franklin System and understanding the Productivity Pyramid, you possess the tools to construct a life aligned with your deepest desires and values.

As Benjamin Franklin himself said, "Dost thou love life? Then do not squander time; for that's the stuff life is made of." Embrace the Franklin System and start crafting your masterpiece – a life that is uniquely yours.

CHAPTER 9

THE GLOBAL LIFE PURPOSE

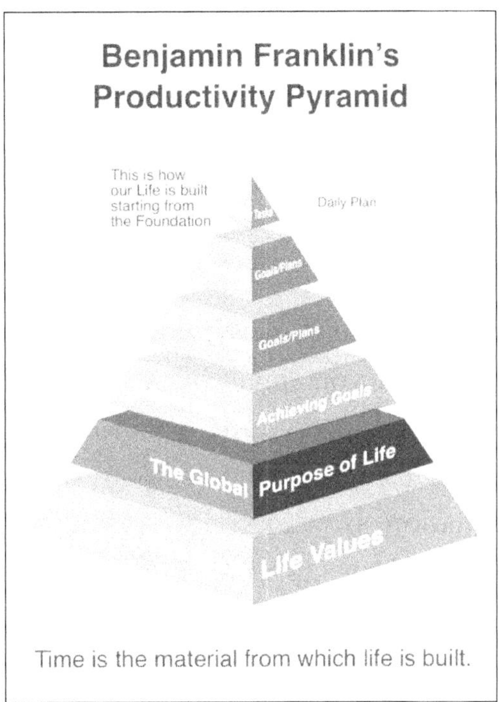

Figure 1.3

This chapter explores the concept of a global life purpose and the construction of the second floor of the Franklin pyramid – the unique reason for your existence. It delves into finding your specific purpose through God-discovery, self-discovery, aligning your life with your values, and also offers a process for finding your purpose. Many cultures and philosophies contemplate the actual purpose of life. Some believe it is to connect with a higher power, while others see it as contributing to something larger than ourselves. Regardless of your specific belief system, there is a universal yearning to find meaning and fulfillment in our existence and in this present life. And there is a level of fulfillment you cannot attain in life unless you are living your purpose, which is the reason you were born. In order to be truly fulfilled, whatever you do with your life, which should be the very reason for your existence, must be congruent with your values. This is the only thing that can lead to lasting peace.

Understanding the Global Life Purpose

The Global Life Purpose is the second level, the second block, and the second floor in the Franklin system. This level two builds on level one. The global life purpose comes from the main values of life or your main life values. In the Franklin productivity pyramid, everything evolves, and each level is built on the previous level, while the main values of life form the solid foundation. If you remain at level one and do not discover and fulfill your purpose, your life will remain like a pipe dream. The global life purpose is specific and requires the description of our mission. It is called a global life purpose because you are dealing with your lifetime purpose, that is, a purpose that will last you a lifetime.

Specificity is Needed

At this level, we are more specific than level one. We should write down our dreams and mission and indicate numbers. We need to take into account specifics. In describing your global life purpose, you must consider anything and everything that will help you describe your purpose in great detail, and you must write it down. We are considering where we would like to be at the end of our life and all the things we would like to achieve with our lives. You must discover for yourself what you are called to do with your life, whom you are called to, where you are called, and how many you are called to reach in your lifetime. Your global life purpose is your life purpose. This is the very reason for your existence.

Are You Lost?

Adam was lost in the Garden of Eden where life on earth started. It is impossible that God did not know where Adam was, for God asked, "Adam, where are you?" "

Genesis 3: 8-10

8 And they heard the voice of the Lord God walking in the garden in the cool of the day: and Adam and his wife hid themselves from the presence of the Lord God amongst the trees of the garden. 9 And the Lord God called unto Adam, and said unto him, "Where art thou?" 10 And he said, "I heard thy voice in the garden, and I was afraid because I was naked, and I hid myself" (emphasis is mine).

Could Adam have been missing in God's radar system? Could Adam have been outside of God's purview? We know that God is Omnipresent, Omniscient. So, why was God looking for Adam? The answer is because Adam was missing in action or location. Adam was MIA. In short, Adam was lost. What does it mean to be lost? Purpose has been described as "the reason for which something is done or created or for which something exists". When we do not know our purpose, we are lost or like in the case of Adam, we are not where God placed us, that is on location or in our area of gifting, we are lost. You are totally lost when you are practicing medicine in a hospital when you are supposed to be a businessman, a fund manager, or an investor. Many are unfulfilled because they are lost. They have not just lost years; they are totally lost.

You Must Touch Your Purpose Everyday

The Franklin system is designed so you can touch your life goal every day. This is a fundamental shift from the usual process of planning. In seeking to organize your life around your purpose, the foundation is built on your main values for living, which are rooted in your calling, mission, and passion. At this second level, we deal with the important question of purpose. At level one, we understand that we were created to please God. This is our general purpose. This is why God created everyone. This is the purpose of the earth: to please God and to fulfill the general counsel of God. You are not to live for yourself; you are not to live for money, your children, your marriage, or things, including your career. Once you realize that your life is meant to please God, which is your general purpose, this level deals with how you will specifically please God, which is your unique purpose. This is a point of confusion for a lot of people.

How Will You Please God?

Why do some people find this confusing? Generally, when you inquire of the average person with an active faith in God unless they have been taught otherwise, they often answer "to please God." This is our general purpose and the purpose of the earth. It is the primary reason why God created us and placed Adam and Eve in the Garden of Eden. However, your Global Life Purpose represents God's unique vision for your life. The law of purpose is one of the fundamental laws of the universe. In Level two, it becomes personal, deeply personal. How will you please God? What is your unique purpose and personal platform to navigate your earthly journey towards a divine conclusion? In my book *Understanding the Laws of the Universe*, I define the Law of Purpose as "Everything on earth was created intentionally and with a specific purpose." Your Global Life Purpose is the specific reason you were sent into this world. There is a purpose behind everything. For instance, why did God create the Pharaoh of Egypt in Moses's time, who perished with his horses, horsemen, and army in the Red Sea? Did Pharaoh perish in vain?

Romans 9:17
17 For the scripture saith unto Pharaoh, Even for this same purpose have I raised thee up, that I might show my power in thee, and that my name might be declared throughout all the earth.

God raised Pharaoh to demonstrate His power to the then-known world.

Pharaoh and his army, including horses, horsemen, and chariots, were probably the most advanced military force in the world. And yet, in one night, Pharaoh and his military force perished in the Red Sea. What about the horse? Why did God create the horse? Was the horse created for a reason? Let's consider the nature and quality of the horse.

Proverbs 21:31

31 The horse is prepared against the day of battle: but safety is of the Lord.

Revelation 9:9

9 And they had breastplates, as it were breastplates of iron; and the sound of their wings was as the sound of chariots of many horses running to battle.

Job 39:19-25

19 Hast thou given the horse strength? Have you clothed his neck with thunder? 20 Canst thou make him afraid as a grasshopper? The glory of his nostrils is terrible. 21 He paws in the valley and rejoices in his strength; he goes on to meet the armed men. 22 He mocks fear and is not frightened; nor does he turn back from the sword. 23 The quiver rattles against him, the glittering spear, and the shield. 24 He swallows the ground with fierceness and rage; nor does he believe that it is the sound of the trumpet. 25 He says among the trumpets, "Ha, ha," and he smells the battle from afar, the thunder of the captains, and the shouting.

God created the horse for the day of battle, giving it tremendous strength. The horse defies fear, is not daunted by battle, but rather charges towards the sword. It senses the battle from a distance and rushes towards it. That is the purpose of the horse. Everything is created with a purpose.

The Global Life Purpose pertains to your long-term purpose, which is the overarching and predominant purpose of your life. People often ask, "Is there one purpose for my life?' In essence, is there one reason for my birth? Is there a raison d'ètre for my life? People frequently pose this question because they confuse roles and purpose. The predominant purpose of your life is God's vision for your life and your raison d'ètre. Time is an earthly phenomenon. In Genesis 1:1, the Bible proclaims that in the beginning God created the heavens and the earth. The term 'beginning' signifies the commencement of time and creation. God peered through the passage of time and designated a reason, a vision, and a purpose for your life. You are not only uniquely crafted, but you were fashioned for a specific mission. As per the English dictionary, your raison d'ètre, a French term, is the most significant reason or purpose for someone or something's existence. Once the most important reason for your existence or your purpose is more than one, it is no longer your raison d'ètre. You may do many things throughout your life, but unless you use your life to fulfill your life assignment, your life is worthless.

Acts 20:24 - NLT

24 But my life is worth nothing to me unless I use it to finish the work assigned to me by the Lord Jesus—the work of telling others the Good News about the wonderful grace of God.

Even if you owned the whole world and did not fulfill your purpose, you would still be useless in the eyes of God.

Luke 12:15

15 And he said unto them, "Take heed, and beware of covetousness: for a man's life does not consist in the abundance of the things which he possesses.

Moses was many things to many people, including being a shepherd. He was the son of Pharaoh's daughter, a prince in Israel and a son-in-law to Jethro. He was Zipporah's husband and the father of Gershom and Eliezer. However, Moses' global life purpose was to lead the newborn nation of Israel from Egypt to the Promised Land. The reason Jesus came was to give His life as a ransom for sin. He was manifested to die on the cross and thereby destroy the work of the devil. Paul, the apostle, was created to testify to the good news of the kingdom to the Gentile world. He had a far-reaching anointing. Each person has a global life purpose. This is the reason for your birth and the purpose of your life. The reason it is possible and easy to find your purpose, especially if you have adjusted your thinking, is because your purpose is written in your DNA.

Psalm 139:13-16 -

13 For thou you have possessed my reins: you have covered me in my mother's womb. 14I will praise you; for I am fearfully and wonderfully made: marvelous are your works; and my soul knows it well. 15 My substance was not hidden from you when I was made in secret, and intricately formed in the depths of the earth. 16 Thine eyes saw my substance, yet being imperfect; and in your book all my members were written, which in continuance were fashioned, when as yet there was none of them.

God wrote your purpose inside your DNA, and you were fearfully fashioned and wonderfully made. God Himself is a God of purpose and does all things according to the counsel of His will.

Ephesians 1: 9-11

9 Having made known unto us the mystery of his will, according to his good pleasure which he has purposed in himself: 10 That in the dispensation of the fullness of times he might gather together in one all things in Christ, both which are in heaven, and which are on earth; even in him: 11 In whom also we have obtained an inheritance, being predestined according to the purpose of him who works all things according to the counsel of his own will.

God is working toward a predetermined agenda and declares the end from the beginning; therefore, your life is not an accident.

Isaiah 46: 10

10 Declaring the end from the beginning, and from ancient times the things that are not yet done, saying, "My counsel shall stand, and I will do all my pleasure. "

Purpose is Who You Are

Your purpose is who you are. If you do not know what God has called you to do, consider the equipment God has given you, including your abilities and your talents. What do you have? You were created on purpose.

Why did God create the earth? What is the purpose of life on earth? What is the purpose of the earth? Where do nations come from? Why did God create you? What is the overriding purpose of your life? All these questions pertain to purpose. Purpose is the reason something was created, the reason something is done, or the reason something exists. Like every manufacturer, God is a God of intentionality. He is the God of original intention.

How to Find God's Purpose for Your Life

For those who follow a faith-based path, the question of purpose often intertwines with the concept of a divine plan. God has a purpose for each life. There is the concept of a global purpose. Purpose is seen as fulfilling God's will for your life. To find your unique purpose, you need to embark on a journey of self-discovery and God-discovery. We have mentioned this process throughout this book, which involves a lot of self-education and self-reflection. Some of the most inspired men and inventors were self-educated. John the Baptist was self-educated. He was in the wilderness until the day of his showing. John the Baptist was alone with God, observing, studying, listening, reflecting, and meditating. Bill Gates as well as Mark Zuckerberg both dropped out of Harvard, which is formal education, but they did not drop out of education entirely. They were self-taught and self-educated. To truly discover yourself, which is your unique calling, you need to embark on self-discovery and self-education. You need to observe yourself. Why would you need to reflect and observe yourself? This is because whatever you are called to do is already built within you. You are purpose. You cannot make up or manufacture purpose. Your purpose is already part of your DNA and your basic makeup.

Psalm 139: 13-16

13 For you have formed my inward parts; you have covered me in my mother's womb. 14 I will praise you, for I am fearfully and wonderfully made; marvelous are your works; and my soul knows that very well. 15 My frame was not hidden from you when I was made in secret, and curiously wrought in the depths of the earth. 16 Thine eyes saw my unformed substance, yet being imperfect; n your book all my members were written, which in continuance were fashioned, when as yet there was none of them.

Our frame was not hidden from God when He created us in secret and intricately worked on us in the depths of the earth. God saw our frame, and in His book, all our days were written while we were yet unformed. In essence, God encoded our DNA within us and has a book detailing our lives. Just as Jesus fulfilled the volume of the book written about Him to accomplish God's will, God has a unique plan for each of us. As a result of the above, it is easy for you to discover purpose. In the Church world, there may try to confine callings to the traditional five-fold ministry of apostle, prophet, evangelist, pastor, and teacher, but this is overly restrictive.

Purpose is Who You Are!

Sometimes people of faith are confounded and confused that individuals who do not appear to have faith in God the creator of the universe, or those who are not professing Christians or followers of Christ can still identify and fulfill their purpose. This is a reason why that is entirely possible. Firstly, what you are called to do, which is who you are and why you were sent into the world in the first place, is ingrained in your genetic makeup. Secondly, the cultural mandate outlined in Genesis 1: 26-28 is given to mankind and not only disciples of Christ. Thirdly, God reigns over all and is the governor of the nations, bestowing His blessings, including the sun and rain, to shine and fall upon everyone.

Comprehending the Trinity

In the Christian New Testament, [26]"there are three basic groupings of gifts. All these three groupings of gifts are mentioned in I Corinthians 12:4-6: "There are diversities of gifts, but the same Spirit. There are differences of ministries, but the same Lord. And there are diversities of activities, but it is the same God who works all in all.""

Grouping of Gifts

1. "Diversities of gifts but the same Spirit" (v.4). These are referred to as the Manifestation Gifts and are given and operated by the Holy Spirit. These nine Manifestation Gifts are listed in 1 Corinthians 12:8-10.
2. "Differences in ministries but the same Lord" (v5). These are referred to as the Ministry Gifts and are given by Jesus Christ the Son. These so-called Five-fold Gifts are listed in Ephesians 4:11.
3. "Diversities of activities, but it is the same God" (v. 6). These are referred to as the Motivational Gifts and were given by God the Father listed in Romans 12:6-8.

Understanding Manifestation Gifts

1 Corinthians 12:4-12

4 Now there are diversities of gifts, but the same Spirit.
5 And there are differences in administrations, but the same Lord. 6 And there are diversities of operations, but it is the

---

[26] Parrish, Frank R., ACTS Magazine, International Edition, July/August/September 2001: Introduction to Biblical Gifts, Pg 2

same God who works all in all. 7 But the manifestation of the Spirit is given to every man to profit withal. 8 For to one is given by the Spirit the word of wisdom; to another the word of knowledge by the same Spirit; 9 To another faith by the same Spirit; to another the gifts of healing by the same Spirit; 10 To another the working of miracles; to another prophecy; to another discerning of spirits; to another diverse kinds of tongues; to another the interpretation of tongues: 11 But all these work that one and the selfsame Spirit, dividing to every man severally as he will. 12 For as the body is one, and has many members, and all the members of that one body, being many, are one body: so also is Christ.

The above passage speaks of the Manifestation Gifts of the Spirit given to every man, especially Christians to profit in this life. What are Manifestation Gifts? [27]"Manifestation gifts are spiritual gifts that God gives to people to help them bless others. These gifts are a way for God's Holy Spirit to show His power and bring glory to His kingdom." [28] "The manifestation gifts are *supernatural demonstrations of the Holy Spirit's presence and power"* (from Understanding Spiritual Gifts), and they include words of wisdom, words of knowledge, faith, healing, miracles, prophecy (which can also be categorized as a Motivational Gift), discerning spirits, speaking in tongues, and interpretation of tongues." These Manifestation Gifts are the abilities, equipment, and tools of

---

[27] https://www.curtlandry.com/manifestation-of-the-gifts-of-the-spirit/July 31st 2023

[28] https://neuething.org/manifestation-gifts/used on October 31st 2024

the Holy Spirit given to help believers in life and ministry, and they are not limited to church services.

Understanding Ministry Gifts

Ephesians 4: 1-16

1 I, the prisoner of the Lord, beseech you to walk worthy of the vocation wherewith you are called, 2 **with** all lowliness and meekness, with longsuffering, forbearing one another in love; 3 **endeavoring** to keep the unity of the Spirit in the bond of peace. 4 There is one body and one Spirit, even as you are called in one hope of your calling; 5 **one** Lord, one faith, one baptism, 6 One God and Father of all, who is above all, and through all, and in you all. 7 But to every one of us is given grace according to the measure of the gift of Christ. 8 Wherefore he says, 'When he ascended up on high, he led captivity captive and gave gifts unto men.' 9 (Now that he ascended, what is it but that he also descended first into the lower parts of the earth? 10 He who descended is the one who also ascended far above all the heavens, that he might fill all things.) 11 And he gave some as apostles, some as prophets, some as evangelists, and some as pastors and teachers. 12 For the perfecting of the saints for the work of ministry, for the edifying of the body of Christ: 13 until we all attain to the unity of the faith and of the knowledge of the Son of God, unto a perfect man, to the measure of the stature of the fullness of Christ: 14 so that we may no longer be children, tossed to and fro, and carried about by every wind of doctrine, by the sleight of men, by craftiness, whereby they

lie in wait to deceive. **15** But speaking the truth in love, may grow up into him in all things, which is the head, into Christ: **16** from whom the whole body, joined and held together by every joint, supplieth, according to the effectual working in the measure of every part, maketh increase of the body unto the edifying of itself up in love.

This passage discusses the Ministry Gifts of Jesus, which He gave to certain men and women in the Church to prepare the rest of the body of Christ for the work of service to the rest of society.

Understanding Motivational Gifts

Romans 12:3-8

*3 For I say, through the grace given to me, to every man that is among you not to think of himself more highly than he ought to think, but to think soberly, according as God has dealt to the measure of faith. 4 For as we have many members in one body, and the members do not have the same function, 5 **so** we, though many, are one body in Christ, and individually members one of another. 6 Having then gifts differing according to the grace that is given to us, whether prophecy, let us prophesy according to the proportion of faith; 7 Or ministry, let us wait on our ministering: or he that teaches, on teaching; 8 Or he that exhorts, on exhortation: he that gives, let him do it with simplicity; he that rules, with diligence; he that shows mercy, with cheerfulness.*

Foundational Gifts

[29]"There are seven motivational gifts listed in Romans 12:3-8. These seven gifts, given by God the Father are foundational and relate to our basic makeup. When we closely examining the Greek text itself, we observe that the list of gifts in Romans 12 pertains to how each individual is created. These gifts depict, or characterize, our fundamental motivations - that is, how we perceive, comprehend, and approach life and ministry. These fundamental traits are ingrained in our personalities and were instilled by our Creator. But they are more than just personality traits; they are gifts that our Heavenly Father has given to each of us by His sovereignty." They define a person's fundamental life purpose - in essence, they are connected to our calling, mission, and what drives each person. These are inherent inclinations, encoded in our DNA, gifted to each individual by God the Father's unique craftsmanship, and form part of each individual's foundational gifting. Generally, most individuals will exhibit a "blend", characterized by multiple of these motivational gifts. However, there will usually be one dominant and prominent trait that unveils our primary gifting. These seven gifts are Prophecy or Seer; Ministry or Service; Teacher or one who imparts Truth; one who Exhorts or one who Encourages; Giver or one who Shares; Ruler or Leader; and Mercy or Shower of Compassion. Very few of us are solely characterized by one of these gifts. Most often, each

---

[29] Parrish, Frank R., *ACTS Magazine, International Edition, July/August/September 2001:* Introduction to Biblical Gifts, Pg 5

of us possesses a combination of several. However, there will usually be one of these gifts that is more pronounced.."

At the level of the Global Life Purpose, you acknowledge that although there are several things you can do, you must concentrate on your specific gifting from God. You must focus on your basic make-up, which is inherent in you You must not mistake tools and abilities for purpose. At this second level, you must discover your unique calling, your purpose, and your unique platform based on God's specific design for your life. You must not confuse roles with purpose. There is an overriding and overarching purpose for your life. The reason anybody, including those who may not have an active and visible relationship with God can discover their purpose is simply because our purpose is encoded in our DNA, and it defines who we are.

While specific approaches may vary depending on your religion, some general principles can guide your search:

1. God-discovery and Self-discovery: Devote time to prayer and self-reflection. Ask God to reveal your purpose and listen for guidance through scripture, nature, or even other people. 2. Ministry or Serving: It is crucial to position yourself in the place and position where your gifts and purpose can be expressed. God gave us the motivational gifts so we can serve. However, these gifts also shape our fundamental nature. In essence, this is who we are. Therefore, the more we seize the opportunity to serve others, the more our gifts will manifest,

and the more we will understand ourselves. Serving those around us and aiding those in need can be a meaningful way to connect with our purpose and find fulfillment.

3. Living according to your deepest convictions: Align your actions with your core values and inner drives. This alignment between your beliefs and actions can be a significant indicator of being on the right path.

2 Timothy 1:9

Who has saved us and called us with a holy calling, not according to our works, but according to His own purpose and grace, which was given to us in Christ Jesus before the world began (emphasis mine),

The word translated as "world" in 2 Timothy 1: 9, means "time" in the Greek language. The above passage means that God called us with a holy calling according to His own purpose before time began and gave us grace in Christ Jesus, by which He enables us to fulfill that calling.

In searching for your global life purpose, you must contemplate and address certain questions:

The Seven Movement Questions

In the Workbook on *How To Find Purpose*, I share the seven movement questions. What is a movement question? [30]"A movement question is something that prompts you or drives

---

[30] Enelamah, John C., *How To Find Purpose: Applying the Law of Purpose*, JEM Publishing 2024, Pg 60

you towards your eternal or divine destiny." By eternal, we are referring to that which was before time began, and by divine, we are referring to that which is according to the counsel of God.

Here are the Seven Movement Questions:

1. What moves you for free? What do you do that money and time do not matter? What do you do that money or how much you will be paid is not the driving force? What do you do that you don't care about the money, and you are not doing it for the money? What do you do that time passes by with little notice? What do you do that you don't remember time, or if you have even eaten?

2. What moves you for fun? What do you do that you really enjoy doing? What do you do that you continue doing even when you are tired? If you had your way in this life, what would you do with your life? What is your hobby? What do you consider your hobby? What do you do that brings you so much joy?

3. What moves you like fire?
   What are you passionate about? What do you have a passion to do? What are you inwardly motivated to do? What ignites you like fire?

4. What moves you to fitness?
   What are you fitted for? What are you designed to accomplish? What are you inwardly motivated to do? What comes to you naturally?

5. What moves you to fury?

What angers you? What provokes you to anger? What infuriates you? What are you burdened about and concerned about that others do not necessarily share the same sentiment? What gets your blood pumping? What is it that, when you remember it, compels you to go out there and make a difference?

6. What moves you to fulfillment?

    What do you do that brings you inner satisfaction? What do you do that gives you a sense of fulfillment? What do you do that brings you tremendous pleasure? What do you do that brings you joy, inner joy?   What do you do that gives you a sense of destiny and fulfillment? What do you do that makes your life worth living? What do you do that fuels your risk-taking ability? What do you do that you are willing to bet your whole life on?

7. What motivates you for first?

    What do you do that you can be ranked in the world among the best? What do you do that you can be the best in the world at? What do you do that, when you do it, you are full of creative ideas? What could you spend the rest of your life doing that you are uniquely created to do? In this life, your greatness is not in your similarity or your conformity, but in your difference. This is called the Law of Difference. While you should respect and value others, you must remember that you are uniquely created by God.

If you do not know why God created you and have not discovered your purpose, then commit to reading the two books I have written on purpose:

1. The Concept of a Life Purpose

2. How to Find Your Purpose - A workbook.

What Do You Do With God's Purpose for Your Life?
There are five things you must do about purpose: find purpose; focus on purpose; follow purpose; fulfill purpose, and finish purpose. Once you have a sense of your purpose, use it to set your goals. You must align your goals with your purpose to ensure you are moving in the direction that will bring lasting meaning and fulfillment. However, to set the right goals, you will have to develop a general plan for achieving those goals.

CHAPTER 10

GENERAL PLAN FOR ACHIEVING GOALS

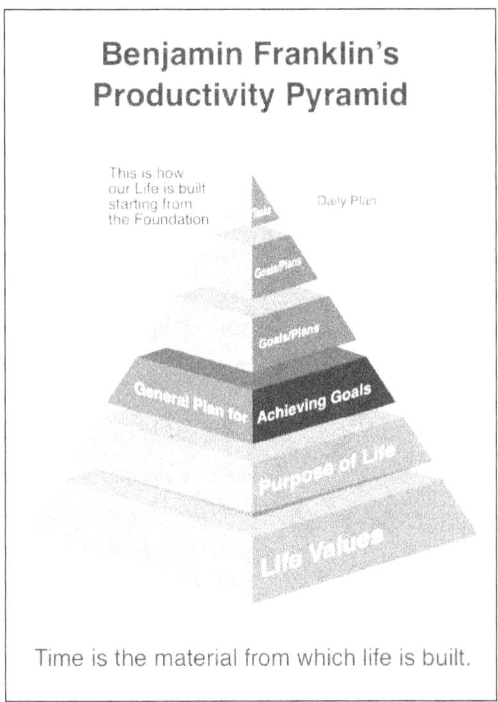

Figure 1.4

Each person must develop a framework to translate purpose into action. In this chapter, we are discussing the General Plan for Achieving Goals, which is a master plan for achieving your life goals. This is the third floor and level three in the Franklin System and deals with methods and tools. The objective of planning our lives is to organize our life around our life goal, which is our purpose. Organizing is a skill that is required to plan effectively.

At this level of the Franklin system, having determined,

discovered, and defined your purpose, you will need to settle down and plan. Once you understand what you are called to do with your life, you will need to determine what you will need to accomplish the vision and what you have to accomplish this God-given vision. When we have a dream, we must break it down into concrete steps. Every step must take us closer to our goal and our dream and should direct us on how to achieve the desired result. You have to count the cost of fulfilling God's plan and be willing to pay the price. Every calling has a price tag. Though nobody will ever have all it takes to fulfill God's plan, yet most people underestimate what they have. At the same time, most people underestimate the real price of fulfilling purpose.

Effective planning will require that we engage in a number of activities, including self-assessment: we need to assess what we have. In the journey of self-discovery, we discover who we are, and in the journey of self-assessment, we discover what we have. God asked Moses "What do you have in your hands?" Elisha asked the woman from the wives of the sons of the prophets, "What do you have in your house?" and she answered, "Thine handmaid hath not anything in the house, save a pot of oil." That oil was akin to the two loaves and five fishes and the seven loaves and a few little fishes in the hands of Jesus. It seemed inadequate, yet it accomplished the task. We each have enough to fulfill our life assignment, but we need to sit down and strategize.

What do you have in your hands? Consider how your unique

skills and passions can contribute to the greater good, but more importantly, what do you possess that you cannot see? These are known as invisible resources. When planning, you must look beyond yourself and recognize all the gifts that God has bestowed upon you that you may not currently appreciate and acknowledge. For instance, who do you know? What has God instilled in you that you are taking for granted? What comes naturally to you that you are failing to realize is a valuable asset and a divine investment? A God-given calling and assignment cannot be fulfilled through self-reliance; often, we have more than we acknowledge.

We must take inventory of our lives and our resources. Resources can be immediately apparent and tangible, and other resources are less clear and quantifiable. You should focus on and list your invisible resources. An example of invisible inner resources, which constitute our intangible wealth, includes but is not limited to things like the ability to be focused, social skills, the ability to think strategically, communication skills, paying attention to detail, love for people, passion, computer literacy, an entrepreneurial drive, ability to mobilize people, ability to remember people's names, a desire to wear out rather than rust out, commitment to lifelong learning, intellectual curiosity, acumen for numbers, etc.

In conclusion, discovering our visible resources and uncovering our invisible resources should help us develop a general plan to fulfill our long-term purpose. The general plan for fulfilling our purpose will use all available methods and employ all available tools so we can finish our life assignment. God will not send us into this world without the right equipment; however, we need to prepare and plan. Planning is a learned behavior and requires skills. The more we plan, the more we grow in the needed skill. Jesus said in Luke chapter fourteen, who will build a tower, or which king will go to war without considering the resources that are available to them.

Luke 14: 28-32

28 For which of you, intending to build a tower, does not sit down first and count the cost, whether he has sufficient to finish it? 29 Lest, after he has laid the foundation and is not able to finish it, all who behold it begin to mock him, 30 saying, "This man began to build and was not able to finish." 31 Or what king, going to make war against another king, does not sit down first and consider whether he is able with ten thousand to meet him who comes against him with twenty thousand? 32 Or else, while the other is yet a great way off, he sends an embassy and desires conditions of peace.

You need to count costs, you need to prepare, and you need to plan. What are you called to do? What will it take to do it? What do you possess? You need to organize yourself. Once you have identified your resources and you are clear about your mission, you must set goals. Goals can be lifelong, long-term, intermediate, or short-term.

CHAPTER 11

UNDERSTANDING GOAL SETTING

The fourth level of the Franklin system represents our long-term goals and the plans for achieving them. By reaching and fulfilling these long-term goals, we achieve our ultimate objectives in life. This chapter provides a roadmap for setting effective goals, which include long-term goals that must be broken into intermediate or mid-term goals, leading to short-term goals. Effective goals must have specific characteristics and qualities. Goals must be specific, measurable, achievable, relevant, and time-bound. In this chapter, we explore the importance of aligning your goals with your values and creating a hierarchy of long-range or long-term, mid-term, and short-term goals.

What is a goal?

According to Napoleon Hill, a goal is a dream with a deadline. "Someday I am going to...", will never come to pass. We must form the habit of writing down our dreams and putting a deadline to those dreams; only then can our dreams receive new power. Once we understand time, we will immediately understand that we are playing catch up with time. However, everyone has enough time to do the things that are important to them. Even though each person's timeline will vary, there are certain goals that should be achieved at 30 years and some that should be achieved before you are 40 years. Unfortunately, most of us are not on course with our lives.

Life is a vast ocean filled with all kinds of possibilities, but without a clear destination, it's easy to drift aimlessly. Goal setting, a cornerstone of life planning, provides the map and compass you need to navigate toward your desired outcomes. [31]According to Blair Singer of Blair Singer Training Academy, "Goals... A deciding factor in reaching your highest level of success is setting goals." Singer argues that not setting goals is equivalent to choosing to achieve less. I totally agree with Singer. Setting clear goals will have a huge impact on your life.

Importance of Goal Setting

In Chapter 2 of this book, "Laws of the Universe and Life Planning", we describe the study mentioned in the book, *What They Don't Teach You at Harvard Business School*. The key point from that study was that only 3% of graduates had written goals and plans. This showed that the vast majority of students, despite being in a prestigious program, did not actively engage in the practice of clearly defining and documenting their future aspirations. Also, 13% had goals but not in writing. Unfortunately, the lack of a written plan significantly impacted their results compared to the 3% with written goals. A whopping 84% had no specific goals; a large portion of the class had no clear goals at all, leading to missed opportunities due to a lack of direction and ultimately unfulfilled potential. In this study, we learned that written goals led to significantly higher income. This is a striking

____

[31]https://www.blairsinger.com/goals-a-deciding-factor-to-reaching-your-highest-level-of-success/20ChampionLevelGoalSetting.com., last used by October 31st 2024

finding that the 3% of graduates with written goals and plans to achieve them were earning, on average, ten times as much as the remaining 97% of the class combined. The implication of the study is the importance of goal setting and planning. The study emphasized the power of actively setting goals, taking the time to write them down, and developing plans to achieve those goals as a key factor in achieving success. This chapter explores the art of setting effective goals that propel you forward.

How I was Sold on Goal Setting

On a personal level, I was sold on goal setting a few years ago when my wife traveled to the United States for further studies. A year later, our children joined her, and this led to frequent travels on my part. I eventually joined the Frequent Flyer program of Air France/KLM/Delta, the Skyteam. I was often denied access to the lounge except on the few occasions when I flew Business Class. I was told I had to be of Gold status at a minimum in order to freely enjoy the lounge. I set a goal to reach Gold status in a particular year. In that year, I was part of a team that had a scheduled trip to Israel. At that point, this trip was an annual pilgrimage, and we traveled as a team. We traveled on two different airlines, and neither of them was a member of the Skyteam. However, just before we left for Israel in that particular year, it occurred to me that I would not reach Gold status that year unless I adjusted my travel plans. I eventually made that adjustment and flew KLM and Air France. This meant I was separated from the team, but I achieved Gold status that year. I remember receiving the notification around December 26 of that year that I was now Gold. I was so sold on goal setting that I set the goal to become Platinum the following year, and I achieved it. I subsequently understood that this was not just about flying, but goal setting is one of the laws of the universe. When we set goals, we are inviting and utilizing forces completely outside of our control that are much bigger than we are. We are actually asking God to help us, particularly if the goal is important to His agenda. If you are going to finish your life assignment, you must have goals.

Understand Goal Hierarchy

Goal setting is a cornerstone of life planning. There are four levels of goals:

1. Life goals,
2. Long-term goals,
3. Intermediate goals, and
4. Short-term goals.

Goals are in hierarchies, with life goals at the top. Life goals are sometimes described as long-term goals depending on how old we are and represent all that we would like to achieve in our lives. When you are in your teenage years, your life goal could span more than 25 years and must be broken down into long-term goals. However, long-term goals must cascade down to intermediate or mid-term goals, and then short-term goals. Long-term goals (usually between 20 - 25 years) paint the big picture of our life, while intermediate or mid-term goals (between 15 - 10 years) act as steppingstones.

Short-term goals, which could be annual, monthly, or weekly, provide a sense of immediate accomplishment and keep you moving forward.

Learning to Fulfill Our General Life Plan

At the fourth level of the Franklin System, we utilize the concept and principle of goal setting and planning to break down our general plan into smaller achievable units. In its entirety, our general life plan is abstract and unattainable unless we divide it into segments. For example, where will you be in the next 20 – 25 years? What are your goals for the next 25 years? This is our long-term goal. We need to set long-term goals and graduate them to intermediate goals. This is necessary to make our goals more achievable. Our long-term goals are multiples of our intermediate goals. This is because 20 years is made up of two 10-year periods, just like 30 years is made up of three 10-year periods.

How Much Time Do You Have?

How we break down our long-term goals or plan is a function of our timeline and how much time you think you have left when we embark on the planning process. How old are you, and how much time do you have left? Consider the Biblical injunction of seventy years and if by reason of strength, an additional ten years. If you are to live to the age of eighty years, how much time do you have left? How do you plan to spend your remaining years? When are you most likely to optimize your life, factoring in the fact that you are most likely to slow down as you grow older. So, if a person is thirty years old and would like to maximize their life at the age of sixty, which means effectively he has the next 30 years, his global life purpose would have to be divided into three 10-year intervals. However, if you are twenty years old and would like to maximize your life at sixty years old, you have to plan for 40 years. This means you would have to divide your overall life purpose into four 10-year intervals. In designing our long-term plan, we must always consider our current age and how long we need to plan into the future. As already stated, you must consider at what age you intend to optimize your life. Our long-term goal could even be further broken down into 5-year intervals. Both the 10-year and 5-year goals are intermediate goals. What we are attempting to do is to organize our lives around a system that will help us see into the future and make the most of our lives.

The Goal of Life is to Make the Most of Life

Why do we break down goals or why is there a need to break down goals? We are trying to build an organized system, a planned system that will enable us to make the most of our life. We have to remember that time is passing. We must beat death or maximize our life by fulfilling our purpose. We must look into the future and make commitments. You must live your life in a way that you decide how you want to be remembered and what kind of impact you want to have. You have to consider your legacy if you want to literally write your own obituary. The lesson from the life of Alfred Nobel is that by establishing the Nobel Prizes, he not only wrote his own obituary but also decided how he would like to be remembered.

What Is Your Concept of Breakthrough?

Sometimes people have the wrong concept of a breakthrough. They wrongly think that "one day 'something' will happen, and I will have a major breakthrough that will propel me to extraordinary success." Unfortunately, life does not work like that. You have to learn to make the most of your life by accounting for your seconds and, therefore, your minutes, hours, and days. We must live in the moment. To maximize your life, you have to seize opportunities. If you are going to seize opportunities, you have to seize the opportunity that is before you. This is what my friend Ije Nwokorie, the Chief Executive Officer of Dr. Martens Inc. calls "smashing the thing in front of you."

What Is the Flywheel Effect?

The flywheel effect occurs when small wins for your business build on each other over time and eventually gain so much momentum that growth almost seems to happen by itself – similar to the momentum created by a flywheel on a rowing machine. But the flywheel effect is also true for our individual lives. We must live for the moment and make the most of every opportunity in life. According to Jim Collins in his famous book *Good To Great,* good to great comes about through a cumulative process—step by step, action by action, decision by decision, turn by turn of the flywheel—that adds up to sustained and spectacular results.

What We Do Today Will Determine Our Tomorrow

What we do today will determine our tomorrow. We must set goals and make plans to achieve them. You will need to set goals based on your overall life purpose. You will need to determine what you want out of this life. Your goals will flow from your values and your purpose. What are you called to do? What are you trying to achieve with your life? What kind of legacy would you like to leave? For example, if you are called to preach the gospel of the kingdom to the ends of the earth, then you must prepare and be equipped. You have to make important decisions, including what platform you need, the kind of equipment you need, where and how you will acquire necessary leadership skills, and develop the ability to form and manage teams, and how to become an expert in your chosen field. To be a leader, you must first be a servant. Where will you serve, and how will you serve? Those are important goals you must set for yourself. You have to start with long-term goals, which could be as long as 25 years or even longer.

CHAPTER 12

LONG-TERM GOALS

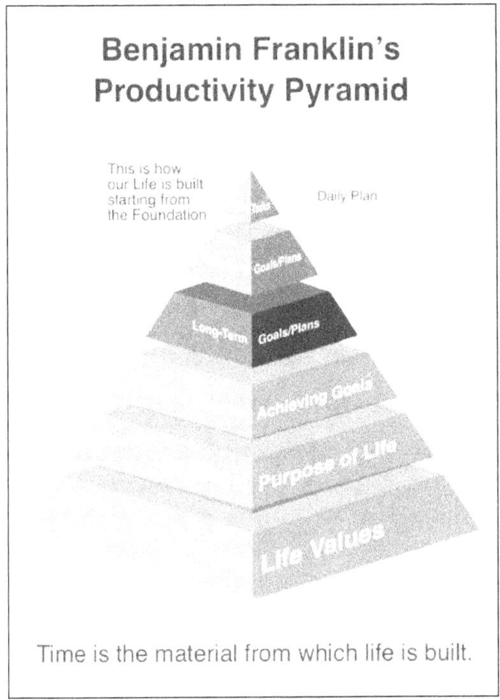

Figure 1.5

What Are Long-Term Goals?

Long-term goals represent the fourth level of the Franklin system and are built on the general plan for achieving goals. If our lifetime goal, our general plan based on our global purpose, is to eat an entire elephant, to effectively eat the elephant, you must consider breaking it down into smaller units and then further into smaller pieces. Eating the whole elephant is your lifetime goal or general plan, and eating the elephant chunk by chunk is our long-term plan. Eating the elephant piece by piece is our intermediate plan, and eating the elephant slice by slice is our short-term plan.

Life planning is the process of organizing and structuring our lives around our life goals. A long-term goal is an ultimate objective meant to be achieved through a series of smaller goals over a long period, covering five to 10 to 25 years or more. A major and distinguishing component of the Franklin system is that it cascades from long-term planning and intermediate plans or goals through short-term goals or plans to your daily tasks or daily plans. While many life planning models start with planning your day, the Franklin system is powerful and very effective because it ends with your day.

Your life goals essentially represent your ultimate aspirations. These life goals must be broken down into long-term goals. While long-term goals may involve major personal achievements or accomplishments, including attaining major milestones, the goal of the Franklin system is that you touch your life every day. Intermediate goals help bridge the gap between long-term goals and short-term actions. Intermediate goals could involve acquiring specific skills, completing educational programs, or saving for a down payment on a house. These are stepping stones toward your long-term goals. The principle is that you will need to break down your long-term aspirations of 20 - 25 years or even longer into smaller, more achievable milestones within a 10-year to 5-year time frame.

The Need to Set Long-term Goals

Planning is the allocation or assignment of activities to our time. Unless we are clear about our purpose and realize the brevity of life, we are not likely to develop a sense of urgency about life. The primary way to develop a sense of urgency about life is by setting effective goals and pursuing them.

How to Set Effective Goals for Your Life

At the base of the Franklin system are our governing life values, which are our main values for living. Your global life purpose is built on your governing life values. Your general plan for achieving your goals is built on top of your global life purpose. On top of your general plan are your long-term goals. In order to set effective long-term, long-range goals, we must be clear about our purpose. Your purpose represents who you are and is a function of what you have been sent to accomplish in this life. When I was younger, I had a recurring dream that lasted for a number of years. I recounted this dream and this season of my life in my book *The Concept of a Life Purpose.*

[32]"Many years ago, I lived in Scranton, Pennsylvania, and I had a recurring dream. This dream lasted for a long season. In this dream, I would often find myself in a classroom setting in an examination scenario. I repeatedly noticed that though I knew the materials (the subject matter), I was often not able to produce the best results. I was either late,

---

[32] Enelamah John C, *The Concept of a Life Purpose: How to Find and Fulfill Your Global Life Purpose*, AiMP Publishing, Lagos Nigeria 2021, pg 130;

distracted, or something always went wrong. This dream was repeated often and looked very abstract. It took me many years to understand the meaning and to interpret this recurring dream accurately.

It was about life and preparation. It depicted my life and the lack of preparation. Life is a test, and I needed to be prepared. You can delay your destiny by the level of your preparation or lack of preparation thereof. I underestimated the price of success. There is nothing significant on earth that does not have a price tag. I have had to put on a battle mentality and develop a Growth Mindset that is ready to work. Though I have always had a sense of destiny, nobody can honestly tell you the story of maximizing destiny until they have done it. Like Paul the apostle stated in his letter to the Corinthian church, everyone who strives for mastery must go into strict training and develop self-control in every area of their lives (1 Corinthians 9: 25). The key phrase here is 'going into strict training'."

The reason I misread the above season of my life was because I lacked a sense of time, which is a sense of urgency. This was because I did not understand time and timelines. I was in my twenties, and I thought I had a lot of time on my hands. I actually thought I was young and that there was no need to hurry. I did not understand that in God's calendar for my life, time was ticking, and there were many things I was leaving undone simply because I did not understand how life worked. I had no written long-term goals and did not even understand the importance of this season of my life. Many are making the same mistake that I made." There are some who are in their thirties who still think they are young, whereas they should have launched into the depth of their calling. They still have not discovered their mission in life, and they are not actively seeking to find their place in the grand scheme of things. They simply think that they are young. However, Joseph became Prime Minister of the ancient kingdom of Egypt at the age of thirty, David became king of Egypt at the age of thirty, and Jesus was about thirty years of age when he launched into His life mission. Being thirty is not being young in God's calendar for humanity. In his autobiography "*Expect a Miracle: My Life and Ministry*", Oral Roberts, who founded Oral Roberts University, wrote that as he approached the age of thirty, things came to a climax. He realized that it was time to take the healing ministry to his generation, and yet he realized how unprepared he was. Roberts was compelled to enter into a long fast that set him on a collision course with destiny and ultimately altered the course of his life. According to Roberts, how long he fasted, he could not remember, but he fasted long enough that he lost so much weight and could no longer fit into his old clothing. What was the result? Roberts had a close encounter of the God kind. God delivered his life purpose to him and gave him instructions that influenced the rest of his life and laid the foundation for the founding of Oral Roberts University.

Lessons From Benjamin Franklin

Benjamin Franklin was America's self-improvement expert. "Benjamin Franklin, a champion of personal productivity, once said, "Doest thou love life? Then do not squander time, for that is the stuff life is made of.""[33]

Benjamin Franklin as one of the Founding Fathers of the United States, achieved so much more in his lifetime. During Franklin's 84 years alive, he invented the lightning rod, made significant discoveries in physics and population studies, wrote best-selling books, composed music, and played the violin, harp, and guitar at a high level, founded many civic organizations, including the University of Pennsylvania, and much more. How did Franklin achieve so much more than his contemporaries, given that he had the same 24 hours each day to get things done? The answer to this question lies in Franklin's daily schedule. Here's how it works, including 10 lessons that will double your productivity this week.

Effective Goal Setting is a Multi-Step Process

Effective goal setting starts with identifying your values. Before you can set effective goals, you must reflect on your core values. You have to ask the question, "What matters most in my life?" This question will help you clarify your mission, calling, and passion, ultimately leading to the discovery of your global purpose. Your global purpose is essentially the reason you were sent into this world. To fulfill

---

[33] Winwood, Richard I, *Time Management: An Introduction to the Franklin System*, Franklin International Institute, Inc. 1990, pg 13

this purpose, you must develop a general plan. Effective goal setting will align your goals with your values in a way that will ensure that you lead a life that is congruent and empowers you to live a meaningful and fulfilling life that achieves your highest aspirations. Effective goals are not only empowering, but they are SMART: Specific, Measurable, Achievable, Realistic and Time-bound. Specificity provides clarity, while the ability to be measured allows you to track progress. Being achievable keeps you motivated, and being realistic ensures the goal aligns with your values, while a defined time frame creates a sense of urgency.

CHAPTER 13

Short-term Goals

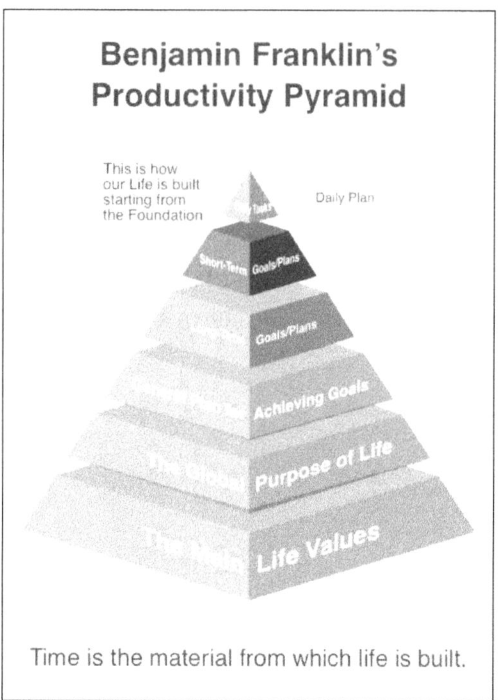

Figure 1.6

Short-term goals or short-term plans depicted in Figure 1.6 form the fifth level in the Franklin system. Since a goal is a dream with a deadline, every goal should have a deadline.

There are four categories, and they are as follows:

- Life goals: these are life-sized goals you hope to achieve over your life-time.
- Long-term goals: these are targets that require 10-25 years or more to achieve

- Medium-term or intermediate goals: these goals span 2-5 years.
- Short-term goals: these are goals that are achievable within a year.

What are short-term goals?

We can define short-term goals as objectives that we can achieve in the near future. Short-term goals could typically be achieved within weeks or months. Generally, short-term goals assist you in making steady progress toward larger, long-term, and intermediate objectives. Short-term goals represent actionable steps that propel you toward your intermediate and long-term goals. These are tasks you accomplish each week or month or within a year that move you closer to your mid-term goals and ultimately, your long-term vision. These might be weekly tasks, daily habits, or milestones achieved within a short time frame like a year. However, doing tasks requires routines.

Why are short-term goals important?

Short-term goals are important for several reasons. Firstly, they form stepping stones to achieving longer-term objectives. Secondly, they also provide a roadmap for achieving success. Thirdly, they help you stay focused and motivated.

[34]"Think of your life as a coloring book. Your long-term goals are the black-and-white outlines on the page. Your

---

[34] https://www.betterup.com/blog/what-is-a-short-term-goal, written December 22, 2023

short-term ones are how you color them in. In other words, short-term goals are crucial to helping you build the big picture of your life. And, just as you would choose the best coloring pencil for the job, your short-term goals should keep you moving forward."

Benefits of Achieving Short-term Goals

There are several benefits that accrue from setting and reaching short-term goals. Firstly, short-term goals are easily achieved; they help us to smash the things that are in front of us, thereby creating momentum. Secondly, we are able to track progress, especially knowing our current position with respect to our longer-term goals. Thirdly, we increase our confidence level by eating the fruit that is right before us and meeting our immediate deadlines. Fourthly, meeting or achieving our short-term goals offers quick turnaround and helps us to overcome procrastination. By setting and achieving short-term goals that are an offshoot of our long-term goals, we will be closer to fulfilling our ultimate goal, which is our life goal. You can use short-term personal goals to achieve these benefits in all areas of your life.

CHAPTER 14

DAILY PLANS

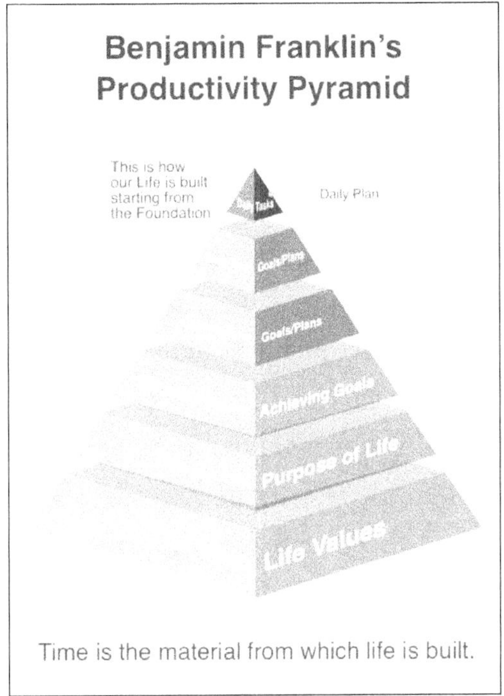

Figure 1.7

This is the final floor and level of the Franklin System, your daily plan, depicted in Figure 1.7. You must plan your day. You cannot live effectively without a daily plan. Daily plans, though not the starting point, are the hallmark of the Franklin system. A fundamental key to effective living lies in how you manage your time. You must plan your day by planning your time. Alan Lakein, a Time Planning and Life Planning Consultant believes that "No matter how busy you are, you should always take the time to plan." Lakein surmises that "The less time you feel you have to spare, the more time is needed to plan your time carefully. Spend only ten minutes at the beginning or end of your day planning, and it will repay your efforts many times over." Planning your day means scheduling your activities and tasks by allocating or assigning tasks or activities to your time.

You must break down your short-term goals into daily plans, and your daily plans must be broken down into routines, tasks, and activities. You cannot do a goal, but you can do a task, which are routines. So, your daily tasks are usually daily routines. Forming and adhering to daily routines is the key to effective living. These routines make up our day. The more predictable our lives are, the more effective we will be in our lives. Our routines represent our habits and make our lives much more predictable. Generally, we dread routines, but routines, which are the boring basics of life, are the keys to long-term achievement. According to Dick Kramer of the defunct Nigerian Practice of Arthur Andersen, and African Capital Alliance, "We first form habits, and then habits form us."

Unless goals are broken down into actionable daily tasks, we cannot fulfill God's plan for our lives. Developing routines and following them ensures you make consistent progress, avoid feeling overwhelmed, and ultimately fulfill your purpose. The other thing is scheduling. While prioritizing implies that we should focus our energy on high-value and high-yielding activities, we still need to build a schedule. If you use the ABC priority system, you must determine which activities are must-do tasks, which are B, which you might do, and which are C, which you should mostly avoid. However, we must remember that our system of valuing activities is subject to human error. What you consider an A activity might actually be a B, and vice versa. The key, again, is flexibility. We must also remember that activities or tasks, which are considered high value and high yielding, may be further divided into A-1, A-2, A-3, A-4, etc. The goal is to complete the A activities before starting the B activities. The principle here is to remember that as long as we have taken the time to think through and rank our activities as accurately as possible while planning our day, it will not matter where the end of the day ends. If we plan our daily work and work the daily plan, we will have made the most productive use of our day. How you prioritize your work is largely influenced by your core life values, which are your fundamental values for living. What may be an A activity for you could be a B activity for someone else. There is truly no need for comparison or competition.

Benjamin Franklin as already stated, was one of the most accomplished men who has ever lived. Franklin strove all his life to attain perfection.

Living Multiple Lifetimes in One Lifetime

In order to make the most of life, Franklin lived his life in blocks. He divided his day into six blocks that ensured he not only maximized his day but also that he was gainfully employed throughout the day. At some time in his early twenties, Franklin conceived the bold and arduous project of arriving at moral perfection. Franklin lived several lifetimes in one lifetime.

According to Franklin,

"I wished to live without committing any fault at any time, I would conquer all that either natural inclination, customs, or company might lead me into. As I knew, or thought I knew, what was right and wrong, I did not see why I might not always do the one and avoid the other."

By the above commitment, Franklin had embarked on a journey of self-improvement that proved challenging but gave him an edge throughout his life. His commitment to self-improvement distinguished him throughout his life and made him one of the most accomplished Americans in early America and in the colonies. Franklin developed thirteen virtues with their precepts and designed his "little book" to keep track of his life. This book proved handy, and living the virtues proved heady.

One of those virtues was Industry. Franklin defined industry as "lose no time: be always employed in something useful; cut off all unnecessary distractions." Franklin kept his daily schedule simple.

Living By Blocks

Benjamin Franklin divided his day into blocks of time. These blocks were as follows:
1. Block 1: 5:00 AM - 8:00 AM - Waking moment and

   preparation for the day.
2. Block 2: 8:00 AM - 12:00 Noon - Work
3. Block 3: 12:00 Noon - 2:00 PM - Break
4. Block 4: 2:00 PM - 6:00 PM - Work
5. Block 5: 6:00 PM - 10:00 PM - Putting things in their proper places, supper, music, or diversion, conversation, and closure for the day.
6. Block 6: 10:00 PM - 5:00 AM - Sleep

In this way, Franklin made the most of every day and ultimately made the most of his life. According to Franklin, he started the day by asking the morning question, "What good will I do today?" and ended the day by asking the evening question, "What good have I done today?" The difference between Franklin's work ethic and style from most people is that Franklin's work time included study, research, and self-education. Though Franklin had little or no formal education, having been apprenticed early by his father, Franklin through self-education, became one of the most educated men in the colonies.

A Game Changer

Benjamin Franklin had two blocks of time in which he did most of his work, between 8:00 AM - 12:00 noon and 2:00 PM - 6:00 PM. However, for Franklin work included reading and research. Though Franklin had little formal education, his reading habits throughout his lifetime distinguished him and eventually made him one of the most educated men in the colonies. Introducing reading, blocking time for it, and taking time to research his work made a big difference in the life of Franklin and in what he achieved over time. In fact, it was a game-changer. This is probably one of the reasons Franklin was also an accomplished scientist and inventor. Part of Franklin 'daily plan was research and self-development, which involved reading and thinking. Franklin was intentional about reading and thinking throughout his life.

Lessons from Warren Buffet

[35]"Warren Buffett, known as the "Oracle of Omaha," is an American businessman and philanthropist, widely considered the most successful investor of the 20th century." He has made billions for decades. He is excellent at what he does. According Warren Buffett's [36]80% rule: The most successful people spend a great deal of time reading and thinking. The irony is that he rarely makes decisions. And when he does, he is in it for the long haul. He likes to buy and hold "forever". And before he invests, he reads a lot of annual reports. A lot of them. He likes to be informed before he buys and holds for eternity. And that process also involves a lot of thinking too. Though the most successful investor of our time, how does Warren Buffet spend his day? How has Warren Buffet spent most of his career? Warren Buffet has spent 80% of his career reading and thinking. He takes reading to the extreme. And that habit has paid off for decades. How do you spend your day? Like Buffet and Franklin, do you spend time to read and think? Spending time to read and think should be an important part of your

---

[35] https://www.britannica.com/money/Warren-Edward-Buffett, Updated: November, 02, 2024

[36] https://www.theladders.com/career-advice/warren-buffetts-80-rule-the-most-successful-people-spend-a-great-deal-of-time-reading-and-thinking?utm

daily plan. However, to achieve this, you must avoid distractions.

Dealing with Distractions

What is a distraction? A distraction represents any activity you can avoid that you are currently engaged in. Distraction can also mean accepting roles and assignments that you don't need or that others can handle. As much as lies within your power, you should focus your energy on those roles and activities only you can handle. This may only be possible as you grow in your calling and purpose. Distractions can also be unwanted interruptions to work, like people stopping by your desk to chat during important work time. If you are going to reach your life goal and fulfill your purpose, you must avoid distractions like a plague by minimizing or eliminating them completely. Distractions are not measured by the importance of the role but rather by the necessity of the role. For example, you should not do for yourself what others can do for you. This means you must learn the important management principle of delegation. Distractions represent one of the biggest challenges to productivity and peak performance. During your peak hours, you must take active steps to minimize potential interruptions and focus on your most important tasks.

Techniques for Avoiding Distractions

Some techniques for dealing with distractions include:

1. Minimizing the use of your handset: Our handsets are likely to pose the greatest challenge to our productivity. Unfortunately, we own our handsets, and they belong to us. This means we carry them everywhere we go. They

seem so important that you are likely to wonder how you lived without them. However, we must remember it is a matter of personal discipline. Like Paul the Apostle, we must discipline ourselves. You have to live your life in a way that your handset fulfills its purpose of being a tool of communication, that is, to make and receive calls or to communicate by texting or WhatsApp messaging. It must not be for idling away.

2. Learn to use apps: you can, and you should employ the services of apps that help you turn off your phones or put them in silent mode, or simply put your phones away during important work times. Phones can be a constant distraction during times of prayer, meditation, or solitude. You have to control your handset and not let it control you.

3. Blocking A-Time: In addition to organizing your life in blocks, you need to block out time for A activities. You can achieve this by having uninterrupted blocks of time when you are not interrupted. Just like in a hotel room, you can put a 'do-not-disturb' sign on your door, lock your door, or simply inform your secretary that you should not be disturbed at that time. This is important, especially when you need to create time to meet deadlines.

4. Understanding the value of a Second: You have not truly understood time unless you grasp the value of a second. As a teenager in secondary school, our Mathematics teacher, Mr. Nwambekwe, taught us the importance of time when he allowed us to observe the ticking of the clock for one minute, which equals a full sixty seconds. As

a result of his understanding of time, Mr. Nwambekwe emphasized that if you couldn't solve a given mathematical problem within three minutes or so, you either did not yet understand the subject matter or, as the Growth Mindset suggests, you did not currently possess the necessary skills.

5. Running on your Lane: I define purpose as running on your lane. You are distracted when you leave your lane.ne and you do things not meant for you at all. For example, you could get involved in old wives' tales or become a busybody by involving yourself in conversations that are either unnecessary or not your concern. You must study to be quiet and learn to mind your business.

According to the Codecrafter, [37]"In today's fast-paced world, achieving peak productivity is essential for professionals aiming to excel in their respective fields. Whether you're a developer, writer, or manager, recognizing your most productive hours and optimizing your workflow during those times can yield significant results. Here's how you can pinpoint your most productive hours and enhance productivity."

Steps to crafting a daily schedule:

1. Identify Your Peak Moments: According to the Oxford Dictionary of the English Language, chronotype is a term that characterizes a person's natural inclination with

---

[37]https://foysalff.medium.com/maximizing-your-productive-hours-for-optimal-work-efficiency

regard to the times of day when they prefer to sleep or when they are most alert or energetic For instance, are you an early bird or a night owl? Taking the time to understand your specific energy levels and when you are most likely to be at your best will enable you to schedule your most critical tasks during your peak productivity hours. You should know when you are most likely to produce your best work.

2. Plan Your Day: You must start your day with a clear plan. Benjamin Franklin initiated his day at 5:00am by pondering the morning question, "What good shall I do today." He concluded the day by reflecting on the evening question, "What good have I done today." You must spend your waking moments preparing for and planning your day. Remember, the goal is to touch your life goal and purpose every day.

3. Live with clarity: This implies focusing on high-level and high-yielding activities. This means taking those steps and focusing on activities that bring you closer to your life purpose. If you have followed the steps we have outlined in this book to plan your life, your life should be clearer, and you should have a greater sense of purpose.

4. Prioritize Your Activities: There are low-yielding and high-yielding activities. You must systematically eliminate low-yielding activities or, if you must do them, do them at the right time. However, you must focus your life and energy on high-yielding activities. Focusing your energy on what matters is prioritizing.

5. Use the ABC method: Alan Lakein writes that prioritizing [38]"it's as basic as ABC." Lakein introduced and popularized the ABC method. This method works with a daily *To-do list*, which he considers an important key to daily personal effectiveness.

6. Use the Daily To-Do List: Similarly, Alan Lakein believes that the To-do- List is the secret weapon of effective people. Lakein wrote,[39]"People at the top and people at the bottom both know about To-Do Lists, but one difference between them is that the people at the top use a To-Do List every single day to make better use of their time; people at the bottom know about this tool but don't use it effectively."

7. Develop Daily Routines: Develop and practice daily routines. According to Dick Kramer we first form habits, and then the habits form us. A culture of discipline is one of the keys to high-performing organizations with sustained results. [40]Disciplined people who engage in disciplined thought and who take disciplined action---operating with freedom within a framework of responsibilities---this is the cornerstone of a culture that creates greatness. Developing and working with a daily

---

[38] Lakein, Alan, *How to Get Control of Your Time and Your Life*, Peter H. Wyden, Inc./Publisher, Pg 21

[39] Lakein, Alan, *How to Get Control of Your Time and Your Life*, Peter H. Wyden, Inc./Publisher, Pg 62-63

[40] http://www.jimcollins.com/concepts/a-culture-of-discipline.html, last accessed October 31st 2024

routine will have the same impact of greatness on a personal level.

8. Live by Blocks: Benjamin Franklin lived his life in blocks and blocked out time in his daily plan for the most important tasks of his day that move him closer to his goals. You must include high-impact activities, those things that help you stay on the cutting edge like time to prepare for meetings, reading, and research for the work you do.

9. Schedule time for essential activities: Don't forget to factor in time for sleep, meals, exercise, and leisure activities to maintain a healthy and balanced life. Also, block time for A-activities.

10. Leave room for flexibility: Do not schedule more than sixty percent of your time. Since life is not always predictable and throws us curveballs, we must be flexible by scheduling buffer time to handle unexpected events or simply to take a break and refresh ourselves. According to Alan Lakein, [41]"Flexibility is needed to accommodate whatever situation may arise." If you fill every moment in advance with appointments, without any breaks except for lunch, you are bound to go home frustrated, nervous, and tense."

Framework for integrating the Franklin System into your Daily Life:

The Franklin System empowers you to translate your values

---

[41] Lakein, Alan, *How to Get Control of Your Time and Your Life*, Peter H. Wyden, Inc./Publisher 1973, Pg 47

and aspirations into daily action. The following is a framework for integrating the Franklin System of planning into your life:

1. Morning Ritual: Begin your day by reviewing your personal constitution. Reflect on your most important values and goals for the day ahead.

2. Daily Planning: You must develop a daily to-do list. If you use a daily planner, schedule specific tasks in your daily planner, allocating time for activities. Remember the ABC approach.

3. Weekly Review: Dedicate time each week to reflect on your progress and to develop a weekly schedule. This could typically happen on Sunday evening as you prepare for the upcoming week. According to Alan Lakein, [42]"In laying out a weekly schedule, the key is to block out time for the tasks that require a lot of time." Schedule large enough blocks of time to build momentum. Reserve specific days of the week (such as Tuesday and Thursday mornings) for major projects." During your weekly review, you would like to ask certain questions: How did your week go? Did you achieve your goals for the week? Are there adjustments needed in your schedule or priorities?

4. Monthly Reflection: You will need to conduct a more comprehensive review at the end of each month, analyzing how your weekly actions contribute to your long-range, long-term goals. You should make adjustments as needed.

5. Life-long Commitment to Self-education: Benjamin

---

[42] Lakein, Alan, *How to Get Control of Your Time and Your Life*, Peter H. Wyden, Inc./Publisher 1973, Pg 42

Franklin was self-educated. The Franklin System is a lifelong commitment to self-discovery and self-development. You must commit to lifelong learning, and you must write down your long-term goals. You need to carry your personal commitment in your heart and in writing, regularly revisiting it and, where necessary, adapting and making any needed adjustments.

CHAPTER 15

PERSONAL APPLICATION OF THE FRANKLIN SYSTEM

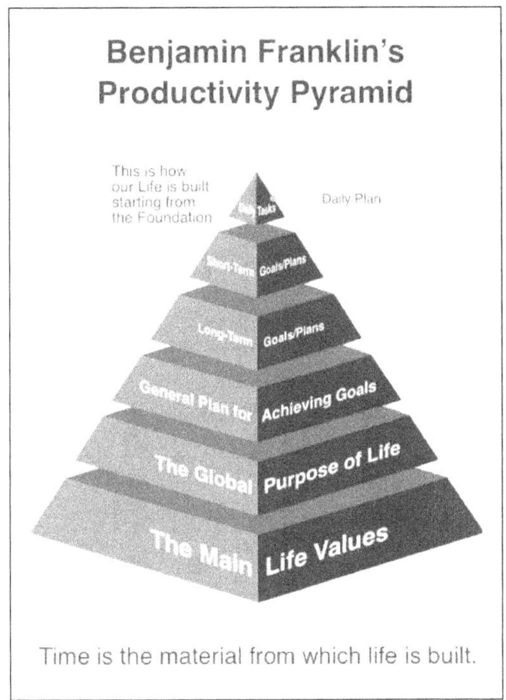

Figure 1.1a

Life planning-based goal setting is a powerful tool for transforming your dreams into reality. By following the steps outlined in this book and integrating the Franklin System based on the Benjamin Franklin Productivity Pyramid depicted in Figure 1.1a into your life, you will be well-equipped to chart your course towards making the most of life. Life is for living. It is not only the years in your life that count, but the life in your years. The Book of Proverbs in the

Old Testament makes a distinction between the *length of day* and *a long life.*

Proverbs 3:1-3
¹ My son, forget not my law; but let thine heart keep my commandments: ² For length of days, long life, and peace shall they add to thee. ³ Let not mercy and truth forsake thee: bind them about thy neck; write them upon the table of thine heart:

According to the Oxford English Dictionary, the word 'and' is a conjunction "used to connect words of the same part of speech, clauses, or sentences, that are to be taken jointly." In Proverbs 3:2, the Bible says, "For length of days, and long life, and peace shall they add to thee." What is length of days? They are the *long days* that make up *a long life.* What is a long life? It is a life that is long on the earth, like Joseph the son of Jacob who died at the age of one hundred and ten, or even Jacob who passed away at the good age of one hundred and thirty-seven, or Abraham who passed away at the grand age of one hundred and seventy-five. Each one of these men lived very productive and accomplished lives. As you know, a day is made up of twenty-four hours. Therefore, a day cannot be longer than twenty-four hours. A long day is a day that is so productive and full of accomplishments that it actually looks longer than twenty-four hours. This is how your day will look when you live a productive life. This is how you can live multiple lifetimes in one lifetime. Each day is full of productive, high-yielding, and high-impact activities that leave you at the end of your day fulfilled and accomplished. Your days are not spent looking back with regret, but they are spent in obedience to the laws of God and the laws of the universe. When your life is productive, your days will seem longer than twenty-four hours, and no two days will be the same. As you come to the end of each day, you don't wait to fall asleep; sleep will catch you. This is because you are spent, and it is usually possible when you have found purpose and are committed to living out your purpose on a daily basis. This will mean that, like Jesus who completed his lifetime assignment in record time, you will be able to say:

John 4: 34 (Paraphrase)
"My food, which *is my nourishment,* is to do the will of Him who sent me. "This *is my purpose within His larger purpose,* and to finish His work, which *is to run my course to a divine conclusion.*"

The Franklin system will not only compel you to discover your governing life values, but it also forces you to discover your purpose, make plans to fulfill it by setting worthwhile long-term and short-term goals, and ultimately live forward by making each day count. Like Zig Ziglar, I believe you must have goals. This is what will set you apart, preventing you from being part of the wandering generality but rather be counted as part of the meaningful specific who find their place in life, change their world, make a difference, leave their footprints on the sands of time, and ultimately fulfill their purpose.

Luke 9:51

And it came to pass, when the time had come that he should be received up, he steadfastly set his face to go to Jerusalem, Jesus was focused, determined, and goal-oriented. He was committed and ready to offer his life for a cause. Should you and I not do the same?"

CHAPTER 16

APPLYING THE FRANKLIN SYSTEM

Sunday Adelaja and the Embassy of the Blessed Kingdom of God for All Nations (The Embassy of God)

Sunday Adelaja is a Nigerian born preacher who built The Embassy of the Blessed Kingdom of God for All Nations, which became the largest Evangelical Charismatic Church in all of Europe by the time he was thirty-three years of age. I first heard of Pastor Sunday in November 2004. In May 2005, I attended a School of Ministry themed "Ministry without Tears, in Lagos Nigeria where he was the Keynote Speaker. We invited him to the Apostles in the Market Place (AiMP) Network, where I was the founding Executive Director through Pastor Mike Adebiyi of Jubilee Christian Church, Atlanta, Georgia. He challenged us to become "an alternative church" and encouraged us to visit Ukraine. I was able to embark on the trip between August and September 2006. The trip was originally scheduled for 10 days but lasted for 21 days.

Objectives of The Trip

The objectives of the trip was to experience firsthand what God was doing in Ukraine in addition to the following:

A. To understand the secrets and principles behind the success of Pastor Sunday and The Embassy of God church;

B. To understand the role of the Church in nation-building;

C. To see how the lessons learned could influence the Nigerian situation.

About the Embassy of God Church

In 1993, Sunday Adelaja began Bible study courses at Kyiv Polytechnic Institute. They held their first public service in February 1994, with John David, a preacher from America as their guest minister. There were 49 people in the first public service. By the first anniversary in February 1995, they already had a thousand people in their church. On September 12, 1994 the church was officially registered at Kiev City Administration. The Joshua Missionary Bible School was opened in 1995 and later became an Institute. In 1995, Pastor Sunday and the church came under the spiritual covering of Apostle Ulysses Tuff. The first graduation of Joshua Missionary Bible Institute was in 1996 and there were seventy graduates. In 1997, daughter churches were started in Kyiv and several new churches were opened in other cities like Konotop, Chernigov. Bright Star Christian Publishing House was founded in the same year. In 2000, the Word of Faith Missionary Center was organized to transform society by preaching the Gospel of the Kingdom. Also, in that year, Pastor Yury Mischenko received a revelation from God to organize nightly prayers for Pastor Sunday and the needs of the church. Evangelist T. L. Osborn, who first visited in 1997, revisited in 2000, strengthening, encouraging, and refreshing the revelation of God. Also, in 2000, the Spiritual

Administration of Evangelical Christian Churches of Ukraine was established, Bishop Anatoly Belonozhko as the president of the administration. All the daughter churches of the Embassy of God came to be associated with the administration. In the same year 2000, Word of Faith Church changed its name to The Embassy of the Blessed Kingdom of God for All Nations. In 2002: Center for Transformation of Business was opened.

Growth of the Embassy of God Church

By the 8th anniversary of the church, over one million people had been saved in the church; over 300 churches had been planted in over 30 countries; 30 services were being held weekly in the Kyiv church (in various auditoriums); and one thousand salvations were recorded monthly at the Embassy of God's Central Church (over 10 thousand per year). Additionally, between 1-2 thousand people were fed daily in the church's "Stephania Soup Kitchen" (almost two million people fed over the past 6 years, and 8th anniversary was celebrated at the Palace of Sports.

The Global Ministry of Pastor Sunday Adelaja

Pastor Sunday has also preached in many nations around the world. The social ministry was launched to bring the gospel directly into different social groups.

Pastor Sunday believes that there are three types of churches:

A. The Traditional Church

B. The Social Church

C. The Online Church

By 2003 more churches were started in Ukraine in Simferopol, Kerch, Cherkassy, Lugansk, Lvov. The Embassy had planted more than 300 churches in cities and villages of Ukraine as well as in the USA, Canada, India, South Africa, Germany, the United Arab Emirates, Latvia, Israel and Holland. In 2005, they held several conferences with the participation of Tony Nwisi from London for the businessmen in the church. As his influence grew, Pastor Sunday was one of the 7 influential leaders of the Protestant church who were invited by the Israeli government. In 2006 he was invited to the Clinton Global Initiative (CGI) and the following year, he addressed the United States Senate and the United Nations.

Mass Action Through Mass Media

The Embassy of God television ministry used to reach over 100 million homes across Europe, Africa and Russia. Pastor Sunday has written over 100 books in Russian and over 100 books are also in English. Over three thousand people have been set free from drug and alcohol addiction. The Embassy of God embarked on building a 15-20 thousand seat auditorium in Kyiv, and it was going to be the first of its kind in Europe. The Embassy of God church believes in and practices strategic praying. They also teach that the church is not an end in itself but a vehicle for nation-building. In transforming society, you move from the spiritual to the natural. The transformation of society is a process. The marriage between the spiritual and the natural has literally produced an explosion at The Embassy of God Church. The

Embassy of God Church is a church-planting organization. The church is mission-minded and takes time to recruit and train missionaries.

The Missionary Center Crucial to Fulfilling the Great Commission

The Missionary Center is an important dimension of the Church. It is the highest level of training at The God Embassy apart from self-education. The Embassy of God Church teaches packaged evangelism and emphasizes that each person has tremendous potential and a calling from God. These callings are often presented both as NGOs to the government/society, and as ministries in the local church. Each individual is encouraged to discover their calling and own the vision by taking responsibility for their calling. There is alignment with, but not conformity to, society. The result is the transformation of society.

The Goal of Ministry is to Disciple Nations by Invading Society

Pastor Sunday is a transformational leader. In the Church everything is allowed but sin. An atmosphere for creativity and freedom is fostered. The people are encouraged to dream, but they must be willing to research their dream. The ministries so established are both law-based and research-based. They have discovered a winning formula for partnership with the government. They preach the Gospel of the kingdom. It is not egocentric. It fulfills the cultural mandate and is focused on society rather than a personal agenda. As an apostolic and transformational leader, Pastor Sunday taught his people to disciple nations by invading every sphere of society.

How to Measure Growth

Church growth is measured by impact as opposed to numbers alone. They are not detached from society. Breadth follows depth. It takes time to make disciples through a rigorous curriculum-based discipleship process. This process also includes coaching, teaching, training, and mentoring. There is a seven-step approach to discipleship, which includes: Encounter with Jesus; One System of Bible Education; Level for discovering Potential; Level for preparing Leaders; Level for preparing ministers; Pastors preparation School; and Missions' Training School. They emphasize fruitfulness and then multiplication.

One System of Bible Education

There is an established curriculum for developing new converts into seasoned ministers and ultimately into cross-cultural missionaries for those so-called. At God Embassy, they implemented the government of twelve, a system of raising leaders based on Mark 3: 14 and II Timothy 2:2. which led to explosive growth. It had a cascading downward pattern for sharing the vision. Cells do not divide, but growth is multiplied through the multiplication of leadership. Everybody is plugged into the vision. Embassy of God Church focuses on reaching the unreached. Pastor Sunday understood that the command is to go into all the world.

Emphasis is on primary growth and not transfer growth. They go where the sinners are and not the other way around. They shout it from the mountaintop. When people come to the Embassy of God Church, Pastor Sunday believes in a system of spiritual education and discipleship.

A Member-centric Church

At the time of my visit, The Embassy of God had over 200 active ministries led by the members of the church. I visited and interviewed 17 of the 35 key ministries in a bid to understand the inner workings of the Embassy of God Church. In the process, I conducted over twenty interviews with key members of the church and staff, and met on several occasions with Pastor Sunday. I also experienced the first week of the 2007 school year at the Joshua Bible Institute, a major contributor to the success of the Embassy of God Church. Pastor Sunday led the week with a series on Times and Seasons. He emphasized that God is a God of Schedule and that He created man to function in time. God has a plan and a schedule for every life. The key to wisdom is understanding time and seasons.

Releasing the Body Ministry

The principle is for the people to be formed and grounded in their faith. They go through a system of education that empowers them to understand redemption, discover their purpose and potential, and ultimately develop various programs designed to meet the needs in society according to their abilities and calling. At the Embassy of God Church, members are trained to unleash their potential. The emphasis from the pulpit is that you are born with something and created with something. The primary purpose of the local church is to serve as a platform for people to discover their calling, realize their potential, and identify their burdens. Once these burdens are identified, they are released as NGOs to all spheres of society. The ministries at the Embassy are initiated and led by members rather than assigned by the church and its leaders. This marked a significant distinction between the Embassy of God and many other churches worldwide. The Embassy of God Church tackled societal issues with a view to transforming society. This is accomplished through the development of social vehicles to resolve societal issues. These vehicles are presented as programs, and the programs are tailored to address specific societal needs. The programs are both policy-compliant and research-based. According to Pastor Sunday, "I teach my people the essence of life".

There is a Price for Revival and Reformation

Pastor Sunday teaches his disciples from the very beginning of their conversion experience what life is all about. He instructs them, emphasizing stewardship, relationship, and leadership, which entail taking responsibility for oneself and society. As a leader, Pastor Sunday believes there is a price for carrying the torch of revival and reformation. The price includes, but is not limited to availability, that is a man who is available to be used by God; a man of deep spiritual depth, this is the result of a life of fasting and prayer; a man of strategic thinking, which is rare; a man of financial literacy; a man of constructive management; a man addicted to God; a man who can develop others; a man of flexibility, that is capable of change and able to adapt easily; a man who can totally depend on God and on the grace of God; a man who is serious about holiness for you must be holy as God is holy; a man of priorities; and a dead man, that is a man who is dead to self.

Each Member Has a Dream

The Embassy of God was built on the voice of God. Pastor Sunday listens to and obeys God. The people, therefore, take revelations from the pulpit seriously. They are also taught to hear God for themselves and to bring the difficult problems to Pastor Sunday. Pastor Sunday develops the people to pursue their own dreams rather than his own dream.

Missions to the End of the Earth

The Missionary Center is one of the most important ministries of the Embassy Church. It was established in 2002. and represents the highest level of training for pastors at Embassy. It is now a two-week intensive school. The training of missionaries is country and region-specific. At the Missionary Center, they believe there are two types of missionaries:

1. Social missionaries: missionaries called to a specific sphere of society.
2. Cross-cultural missionaries: missionaries called across different cultures.

3. Missionaries to People Groups: The word "ethnos" in Greek, which is translated as "nations" in English, actually refers to people groups. Sometimes God calls individuals to a specific people group even within their own nation.

Systems and Organization Needed for Explosive Growth

Pastor Sunday as the Senior Pastor of the Embassy of God Church established the Spiritual Administration of Evangelical Christian Churches of Ukraine. All the daughter churches of the Embassy of God were organized under this association. Both the Missions Center and The Spiritual Administration were led by Bishop Anatoly Belonozhko. He served as the official head of the church before the Ukrainian Government. They also had a board chairman. The church was structured not as a one-man army. It had established administrative structures. There were spiritual councils that operated at various levels. Pastor Bose, Pastor Sunday's wife, had to rise through the ranks until she first became the leader of the English church and eventually the pastor of the Central Church. Pastor Bose previously served as a choir member, a choir leader, a pastor, and eventually as the pastor of the Central Church.

Pastor Sunday's Philosophy About Ministry

Pastor Sunday believes that the Church is the pillar and foundation of truth in any society.

1 Tim 3:14-15 - GNT

14 I hope to visit you soon. However, I 'm writing this to you
15 in case I'm delayed. I want you to understand how people
who are members of God's family should live. God's family
is the church of the living God, the pillar and foundation of
truth.

Understanding the Gospel of the Kingdom

The Embassy of God preaches the Gospel of the kingdom, and this fulfills the cultural mandate of impacting all aspects of society. They embrace a dominion mentality. Society is categorized into seven spheres: These spheres of society, namely politics and government, business and economy, education, media, spiritual/social; arts and culture, and sports and entertainment, representing the gates into society. To revolutionize society and establish control over a territory, you have to take charge of the spiritual/social, business and economy, and education spheres. Pastor Sunday asserts that as followers of Christ we are the salt of the earth and the light of the world. Salt that loses its flavor or saltiness, or its salt content, is worthless and good for nothing but to be trodden under the foot of men. Similarly, light that fails to illuminate and brighten society and overcome darkness is good for nothing.

Matthew 5:13-16

13 Ye are the salt of the earth, but if the salt has lost its flavor, with what shall it be salted? It is then good for nothing but to be cast out and to be trodden underfoot of men. 14 Ye are the light of the world. A city that is set on a hill cannot be hidden. 15 Neither do men light a candle and put it under a bushel, but on a candlestick, and it gives light to all who are in the house. 16 Let your light so shine before men, that they may see your good works and glorify your Father who is in heaven.

Therefore, a church that is not relevant to society is not relevant to God.

Lessons from The Embassy of God Church

We need to understand that as the church transforms into an equipping center, God will draw people supernaturally to the church. In engaging with society, the church must transition from the spiritual to the practical. In some circles, this is known as spiritual mapping and dealing with the foundations. You must then train the people. Emphasis is on retraining the mind. We are essentially what we think. To transform society, you must instill a new mindset, and you must teach a new value system. If there is going to be a change, there must be a change. Therefore, the greatest work a person can do is working on oneself. The culture of a people is their way of life. To change a people, you must change their culture by altering the way they think. This is the key to personal transformation. Only transformed individuals can transform society. The change must be inside out. This is the primary task of the pulpit. Changing the way society thinks is warfare – the task is to introduce a new value system. To construct a new generation, you must construct a people with new mindsets and a new value system. As the people are transformed, they become agents of change themselves. They no longer strive to make a living. They live life to the fullest because they have discovered their destiny. When a person has found their destiny, they become a force for change that cannot be hindered by adverse circumstances. We must continuously confront the forces of darkness. There is a reason why people behave the way they do. We first confront and dethrone forces of darkness, and then we release men. The men so released must impose God on society.

CHAPTER 17

CASE STUDY - SUNDAY ADELAJA: BUILDING EUROPE'S LARGEST EVANGELICAL CHURCH

Figure 1.2a

1. GOVERNING LIFE VALUES or THE MAIN LIFE VALUES of Pastor Sunday Adelaja: [43]"I compel myself to live the life of Jesus every day." According to Adelaja "My mission is to bring the principles of the kingdom of God to my generation and compel my generation to reckon with Christ. I am to pick

---

[43] Adelaja, Sunday, History Makers Training: How to Plan, Structure and Achieve Your Life Goals for the Next 25 Years. Kyiv, Ukraine, February 2019

up the baton from Jesus whose life was cut short at age 33 because he went to the cross for me. Therefore, every day and in all situations, I live and behave the way He would."

Adelaja's Governing Life Values depicted in Figure 3.1 as The Main Values for Living are foundational. At this level, Adelaja was asking the question, "What are my values?" According to Adelaja, it is being obsessed with God. This is the level of falling in love afresh with God, and being totally hijacked and overtaken by God. According to Adelaja, God is my highest value. I love God with all my heart, with all my soul, with all my mind, and with all my strength (Matthew 22: 37; Mark 12:30). God's kingdom is my highest priority. God is my first priority, and then my family: I love my family, but I am obsessed with God. So, I do not have any idols. I am here to do the will of God. My passion is to please God. I live to please God. I will go where he sends me, even if I have to leave success behind. My obsession is God, not my ministry, not my family, not my children, but to please God. Therefore, I am not living for ministry, and I am neither living for my marriage nor my children. Though I need money, the reason I live is not to make money. I am on this earth to glorify God and to please God. Church is not my life's value, growth is not my life's value, and success is not my value. The reason I live is to be totally committed and dedicated to God. As a result, God is totally committed and dedicated to me. I understand that my faithfulness to God is absolute, and God's faithfulness to me is absolute.

Figure 1.3a

2. GLOBAL LIFE PURPOSE: According to Adelaja [44]"I am called to bring the principles of the kingdom of God to my generation. I am to impart God upon my generation through the preaching of the gospel of the kingdom."

Adelaja said: "This is the level where I discovered my specific purpose." Sunday Adelaja's Global Life Purpose, depicted in Figure 1.3a is God's vision for his life. According to Adelaja "My vision is to continue where Jesus left off, whose life was cut short at the age of thirty-three." Adelaja said; "It is about my life goal. My goal is more specific than my values. I

44 Adelaja, Sunday, History Makers Training: How to Plan, Structure and Achieve Your Life Goals for the Next 25 Years. Kyiv, Ukraine, February 2019

realized that if I wanted to discover my calling, I must avoid religion and change my mindset. As a result of changing my mind, it was possible and easy to discover who I am. Religion teaches that there is only the five-fold calling and purpose as found in Ephesians. However, this is only true for those whose purpose is in the Church."

According to Adelaja:

I adjusted my thinking to find my calling; therefore, I am a happy man. I am living for something greater than myself. Although I have a wife and children, they are not the reason I live. My wife and children are complementary. My wife and children are not my purpose. I am not living for me, and they are not living for me. My wife has her own individual and unique purpose. My global life purpose is my specific assignment. I found out that my calling is innate in me. According to Psalm 139: 13-16, my purpose is encoded in my DNA. I discovered myself through self-development, self-study, and self-education. At this level, I am looking for the specifics. What are the specifics? Whom am I called to? Where am I called, and what are the numbers? What results would I like to have at the end of my life? What memory would I like to leave behind, and what impact would I like to have? How old am I now? At the end of my life, how would I like God to assess me? In Greek this is called metanoia, and it means to change your thinking.

According to Adelaja, his Global Life Purpose was to reach 500 million people. Out of this, there will be 20 million believers in Ukraine, 5 million members of "God's Embassy" in Ukraine. He also had a goal to raise 50 thousand ministers, activists, and to establish 10,000 churches and organizations globally.

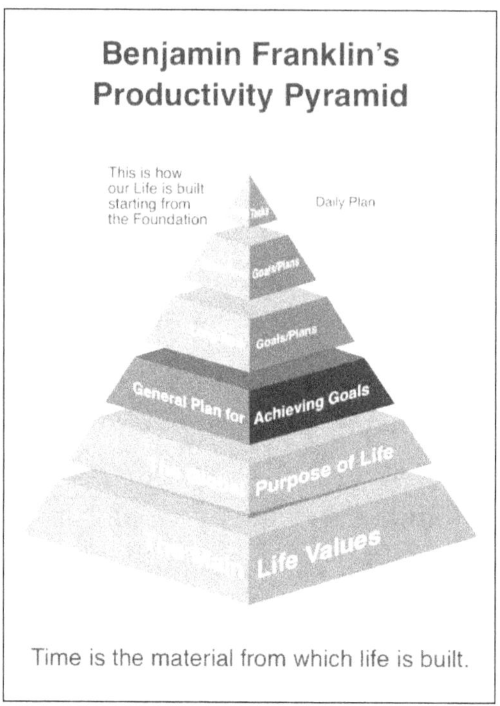

Figure 1.4a

3. GENERAL PLAN OF ACHIEVING GOALS - (Methods\Instruments of achieving goals and inner resources (intangible wealth)

Working with the Franklin system, Adelaja understood that the general plan of his life depicted in Figure 1.4a was closely linked to his global purpose. So, having accepted his global goal to reach 500 million people over his lifetime, the question was, how will Sunday Adelaja reach 500 million people? According to Adelaja, "I needed to break it down into achievable steps. I need to consider what I have. I had to consider what resources were available to me. Where will I get the resources? My resources are like the "two fishes and five loaves." I will never have enough." He understood that the general plan was about resources. So, he needed to reach 500 million people in the next 20 -25 years. According to Adelaja, "I needed to consider what key resources are available to me. What tools or methods do I have? What resources or wealth are available to me?"

According to Adelaja, to reach 500 million people, here are the methods that were available to me: planting churches, raising leaders, mass media, published materials (1000 books), raising socially responsible people, activists, and reformers, raising businessmen, political influence through forming political parties. My methods not only define my life, but they streamline my life. What is the difference between methods and resources? Methods are a set of tools that can help us achieve our goals. Resources are what I have in stock. I realized I have two types of resources or wealth: the visible and the invisible. To reach 500 million people, the most important resources I had were my invisible resources, which are the real riches that God gave me. My invisible resources are more permanent and very reliable. I soon realized that everything God created is from the invisible world.

In Genesis the world was void and dark, and God created something out of it. I decided to be like our Father in Heaven. How? By faith, we understood that the universe was framed at God's command, so that what is seen was not made of what is visible (Hebrews 11:3). The principle is that everything visible was made out of the invisible. How do I practically bring this to pass? I have a vision, but I do not have any money. But the Word was made flesh. According to the Bible, in the beginning, God .... This means for every one of my beginnings, I must find God. In other words, for every new project, I must find God. I am in Kiev now, Father, what would you have done in my place? Between the ages of 19 and 32, although I did not have a concrete plan, I grew. By age 33 I had built the largest evangelical church in Europe. "If you were here, Father, show me the picture. What should I do? Where should I go? How should I proceed? The key is solitude. When I am with Him, I am not alone. I might be in a dilemma, but God is not in a dilemma. In your own beginning, get alone with God. Even though everything was null and void, I wait on God as it was in the beginning when God hovered over the earth. I found a way to focus on God and to move ahead with God. What was the result? The Word was made flesh; that is, the word will come to you. I realized that this was how all of Europe was built. Every inventor, every creative person who has ever done anything great, has been inspired. They have relied on illumination, inspiration, and ideas. It was through bright and innovative ideas that inventors revolutionized their world.

The crucial aspect is translating ideas into words, pictures, and diagrams. Everything visible originated from the invisible; therefore, everything visible emerged from the invisible. What I needed were ideas that I could translate into pictures, diagrams, drawings, and photographs. How do I discover my invisible wealth? What are my invisible resources? As a result of embarking on a journey of self-discovery, I discovered that my invisible resources include passion and obsession with God, focus, a clear sense of purpose, the desire to work hard, commitment to lifelong learning, ability to cast and pass on the vision, ability to think strategically, ability to mobilize people, attention to detail, observant, love for God and compassion for people. I placed the emphasis on my invisible resources, not my physical resources. Out of this came the largest church in Europe and 75 million salvations in twenty years. I also possessed material resources in the form of people, opportunities, influence, and connections. I learned not to walk by sight, but by faith. Though people often complain about what they don't have, the fact is they do know people, have connections, and opportunities. However, the reason people suffer is that they do not know how to turn invisible resources into visible resources. We all have enough riches to do what we are called to do. Each of us is already rich, and we are the wealth we are looking for.

Real riches are not material. We must learn to turn our abilities and talent into wealth. We must recognize all the resources that are available to us, including good looks, diligence, hairstyle, and any other thing we can think of. When the Bible said God blessed Adam and Eve in Genesis 1: 28, it means God gave mankind power, ability, and inner resources to be productive. To bear fruit is to produce after your kind. Essentially, God gave us power to produce after our kind, multiply, replenish the earth, subdue it, and have dominion. So, whatever you want to do, just look within. God has put the ability within because you were packaged for success by God and to excel.

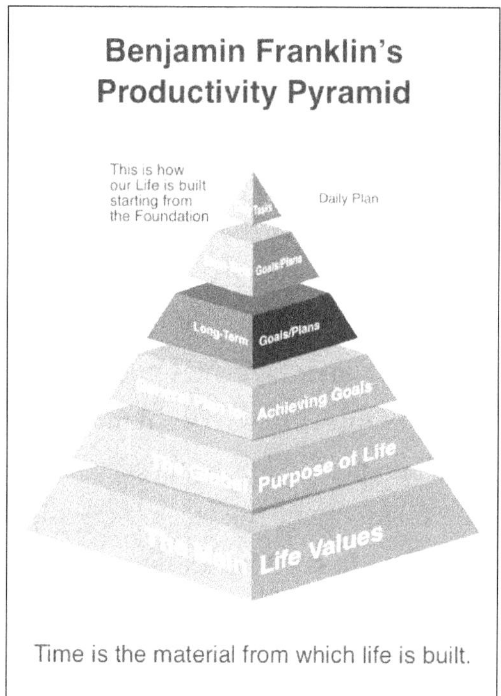

Figure 1.5a

4. LONG-TERM PLAN - According to Adelaja, "my global life purpose encompasses all of my life. But the plan for the remainder of my life is too vast and thus abstract. In planning

to fulfill my global life purpose when I was 32 years old, I realized that it was akin to eating an elephant. How does one eat an elephant? The elephant is enormous, exceedingly so. Therefore, we must consume an elephant in segments. However, we do not commence eating an elephant by consuming small pieces. "We have to start with big chunks, then smaller pieces, and then slices." Adelaja further stated. "Therefore, to make fulfilling my global purpose more concrete, it was necessary to divide my global plan into segments of 20 to 25 years, which were my long-term goals and intermediate goals of 5 to 10 years."

According to Adelaja, "My long-term global goal depicted in Figure 1.5a was to influence 100 million people through television, plant 10,000 churches worldwide, establish Bible schools on all continents of the world, establish Club 1000 on all continents, and lead great healing crusades on all continents." My long-term goals for Ukraine include planting 1000 - 2000 churches, building 300 refuge cities, opening 5000 NGOs and social organizations, influencing 20 million Ukrainians and having 1 million of them as disciples and members of The Embassy of God."

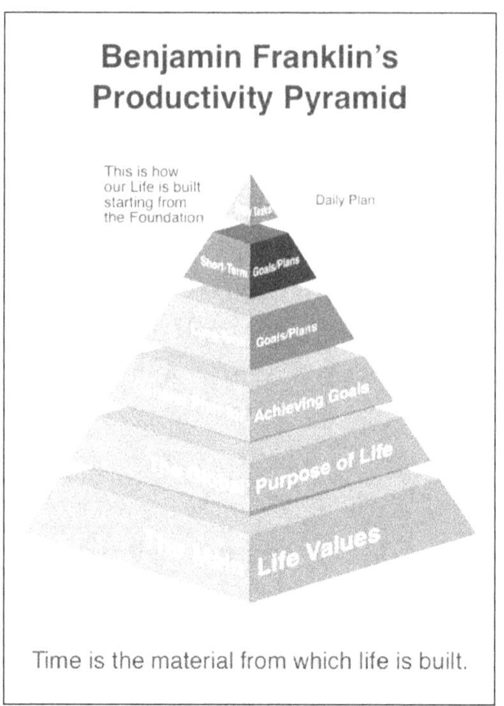

Figure 1.6a

5. SHORT-TERM PLAN - For Achieving Goals (1 week - 1 Year)

According to Adelaja, my main short-term plan depicted in Figure 1.6a is my weekly and monthly routines as Pastor Sunday. These routines consist of my personal prayer retreats, which last for 1 - 2 weeks per month, meeting the apostolic council for 2 days a month. I also held meetings with my regional pastors 2 days a month and meetings with my Kiev pastors for 1 day a month. I also held retreats for selected and qualified individuals known as History Makers Training (HMT). I held the HMT 2 to 3 times a month and led my home groups once a month. I had different home groups. I led and held Anointing Services at the Central Church in Kiev every first Sunday of the month. I also held the Leaders School 2 - 4 times a month. The Leader's School was different from the Pastors Schools held once a year. I also conducted lectures at the Joshua Bible Institute.

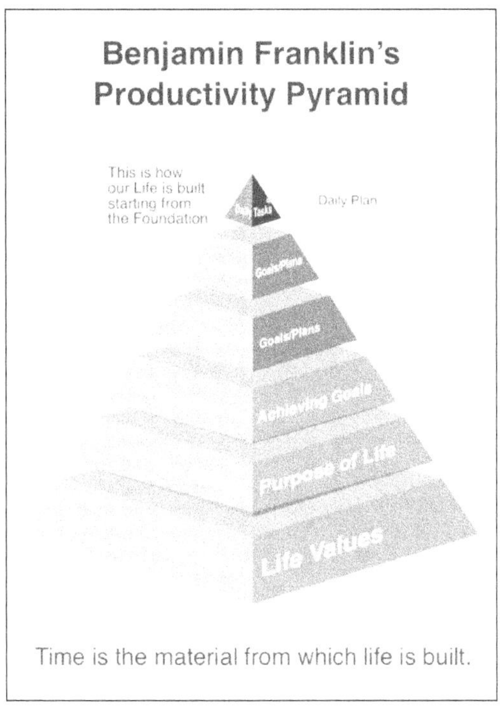

Figure 1.7a

6. DAILY PLAN

According to Adelaja, "my daily plan mainly consists of the habits and routines of Pastor Sunday." Adelaja further posits, "Great people become great, thanks to the restraints, habits, and routines they impose on themselves." Richard L. Kramer, who now belongs to the ages, put it differently. Dick used to say, "We first form habits, and then habits form us."

What are the daily habits of Pastor Sunday Adelaja? The Daily Plans depicted in Figure 1.7a include daily Bible reading, daily prayer, solitude, meditation, research, writing books, spending time with his wife and children, time with staff, daily briefings and meetings, honoring appointments, relaxation, and sometimes watching documentaries. In planning his day, Adelaja states, "Plan not more than 40-60% of the day, and these 60% must be your main routines (main stones)." This is the concept of flexibility as also advocated by Alan Lakein.

CONCLUSION

Time is an earthly phenomenon. As already stated, what you do with your time is what you have done with your life. You manage your life by managing your time. The greatest resource we have is time, and it is given to all men in equal proportion. We each have the same amount of time. Every day, God credits all humans with twenty-four hours, and it expires at exactly 12 midnight. Time can never be stored or transferred to the next day or be retrieved. However, in the Bible we are admonished to redeem time.

Ephesians 5:15-17
15 See then that ye walk circumspectly, not as fools, but as wise, 16 Redeeming the time, because the days are evil. 17 Wherefore be ye not unwise, but understanding what the will of the Lord is.

Ephesians 5:15-17 - NLV
15 So be careful how you live. Live as men who are wise and not foolish. 16 Make the best use of your time. These are sinful days. 17 Do not be foolish. Understand what the Lord wants you to do.

Ephesians 5:15-17 - NLT
15 So be careful how you live. Don't live like fools, but like those who are wise. 16 Make the most of every opportunity in these evil days. 17 Don't act thoughtlessly, but understand what the Lord wants you to do.

What does it mean to redeem time? It simply means to make the most of and maximize every opportunity. We understand this by investigating different versions of the Bible. In this book, by studying the life of Benjamin Franklin and building on the works of several men including Paul the apostle, Alfred Nobel, Abraham Maslow, Richard Winwood, Alan Lakein, and Sunday Adelaja, we can conclude that we can plan our lives. If we adjust our thinking and put on the right mindset, not only can we plan our lives, but we can maximize our potential and therefore our lives.

The Franklin system provides us with one of the best ways to maximize life and fulfill our potential. This system is unique and effective because it ends where most goal-setting and life planning methods start. It ends with the day. [45]"The Franklin system is directed forward - it works with what needs to be done." Why is this effective? Simply because an effective life is the life that takes a long-term view and touches its global purpose every day. Stephen Covey defined this as living with the end in view. According to Adelaja, "the man that trembles over every minute of his life is the freest man." Why would you tremble over every minute of your life? This will only happen when you understand the concept of time. Firstly, everything in this present life is a product of time and is also limited by time. Secondly, you do not have the time to do all you would like to do. However, you have the time to do all you really need to do. Therefore, you need to eliminate all

---

[45] Adelaja, Sunday, System Building: The Key to Resolving Every Problem and Attaining Every Goal, Golden Truth Publishing 2019, Pg 183

distractions and approach the rest of your life with a laser focus. Thirdly, everyone has lost time, so essentially most of us are playing catch up. Therefore, you cannot afford to lose further time. We must seize the opportunity in the lifetime of the opportunity. Like they say, we either play big or we go home. You cannot afford to waste your life. An unplanned life is a wasted life. Go forward and change your world!

ENDNOTES

1. https://www.linkedin.com/pulse/what-top-3-harvard-mbas-did-become-rich-you-can-do-too-dan-stern/November 11, 2015

2. https://en.wikipedia.org/wiki/A. A. Allen, last edited on July 28, 2024 by 4:28 (UTC)

3. Allen, Asa A., *The Price of God's Miracle Working Power*, HopeFaithPrayer Blog, Accessed October 31st, 2024, Pg 70

4. Enelamah, John C., *The Possibilities of Prayer*, JEM Publishing 2021, Pg. 18

5. https://www.siffordsojournal.com/2009/09/davids-digest-introduction-to-type-and-antitype-typology-in-bible, Updated: Thu, 07/20/2023 - 06:04

6. Franklin, Benjamin, The Autobiography of Benjamin Franklin, Yale University Press 1964, p. 157

7. MOGOS: Mission, Objectives, Goals, Strategy

8. Winwood, Richard, I., *Time Management: An Introduction to the Franklin System,* Franklin International Institute, 1990, Pg 5

9. Franklin, Benjamin, The Autobiography of Benjamin Franklin and Other Writings, Penguim Classics 1986, Pg 82

10. Franklin, Benjamin, *The Autobiography of Benjamin Franklin*, Yale University Press 1964, Pg 149 - 150.

11. Franklin, Benjamin, The Autobiography of Benjamin Franklin and Other Writings, Penguim Classics 1986, Pg 82

12. Franklin, Benjamin, The Autobiography of Benjamin Franklin and Other Writings, Penguim Classics 1986, Pg 84

13. https://www.theladders.com/career-advice/lessons-from-benjamin-franklins-daily-schedule-that-will-double-your-productivity, May 30, 2019

14. https://en.wikipedia.org/wiki/Abraham_Maslow, last edited October 31st 2024 by 4:14 (UTC)

15. https://www.biologyonline.com/dictionary/pyramid-of-productivity, last updated on February 24th, 2022

16. *Winwood, Richard I., Time Management: An Introduction to The Franklin System, Franklin International Institute 1990, Pg 36*

17. https://theconversation.com/the-extraordinary-life-of-alfred-nobel, published on Oct 11, 2024, at 8:04 am

18. https://en.wikipedia.org/wiki/Nobel_Prize#:, Page last updated on October 22, 2024 by 6:54 am (UTC)

19. https://www.britannica.com/topic/Nobels-will, Oct. 12, 2024, 9:52 AM ET (AP)

20. https://en.wikipedia.org/wiki/Nobel_Prize#:, Page last updated on October 22, 2024 by 6:54 am (UTC)

21. Enelamah, John C., Striving for the Mastery: Lessons from the Life of Paul, JEM Publishing 2016, Pg 10-11

22. *Winwood, Richard I., Time Management: An Introduction to The Franklin System, Franklin International Institute 1990, Pg 44*

23. *Winwood, Richard I., Time Management: An Introduction to The Franklin System, Franklin International Institute 1990, Pg 45*

24. Winwood, Richard I, *Time Management: An Introduction to the Franklin System,* Franklin International Institute, Inc. 1990, pg. 37-38

25. Smith, Hyrum W., *The Three Gaps: Are You Making A Difference,* Berrett-Koehler, Inc. 2015, pg. 36

26. Smith, Hyrum W., *The 10 Natural Laws of Successful Time and Life Management: Proven Strategies for Increased Productivity and Inner Peace,* Warner Books, A Time Warner Company 1994 1, pg. 46

27. Winwood, Richard I, *Time Management: An Introduction to the Franklin System,* Franklin International Institute, Inc. 1990, pg. 45

28. Parrish, Frank R., *ACTS Magazine, International Edition, July/August/September 2001:* Introduction to Biblical Gifts, Pg 2

29. https://www.curtlandry.com/manifestation-of-the-gifts-of-the-spirit/July 31st 2023

30. https://neuething.org/manifestation-gifts/used last on October 31st 2024

31. Parrish, Frank R., *ACTS Magazine, International Edition, July/August/September 2001:* Introduction to Biblical Gifts, Pg 5

32. Enelamah, John C., *How To Find Purpose: Applying the Law of Purpose*, JEM Publishing 2024, Pg 60

33. https://www.blairsinger.com/goals-a-deciding-factor-to-reaching-your-highest-level-of-success/20ChampionLevelGoalSetting.com., last used on October 31st, 2024

34. Enelamah John C, *The Concept of a Life Purpose: How to Find and Fulfill Your Global Life Purpose*, AiMP Publishing, Lagos Nigeria 2021, pg 130;

35. Winwood, Richard I, *Time Management: An Introduction to the Franklin System,* Franklin International Institute, Inc.1990, pg 13

36. https://www.betterup.com/blog/what-is-a-short-term-goal, December 22, 2023

37. https://foysalff.medium.com/maximizing-your-productive-hours-for-optimal-work-efficiency-c6baeffe3ff8, used on October 31st 2024

38. https://www.britannica.com/money/Warren-

Edward-Buffett, Updated: November, 02, 2024

39. https://www.theladders.com/career-advice/warren-buffetts-80-rule-the-most-successful-people-spend-a-great-deal-of-time-reading-and-thinking?utm

40. Lakein, Alan, *How to Get Control of Your Time and Your Life*, Peter H. Wyden, Inc./Publisher 1973, Pg 21

41. Lakein, Alan, *How to Get Control of Your Time and Your Life*, Peter H. Wyden, Inc./Publisher 1973, Pg 62-63

42. http://www.jimcollins.com/concepts/a-culture-of-discipline.html, last assessed October 31st 2024

43. Lakein, Alan, *How to Get Control of Your Time and Your Life*, Peter H. Wyden, Inc./Publisher 1973, Pg 47

44. Lakein, Alan, *How to Get Control of Your Time and Your Life*, Peter H. Wyden, Inc./Publisher 1973, Pg 42

45. Adelaja, Sunday, History Makers Training: How to Plan, Structure and Achieve Your Life Goals for the Next 25 Years. Kyiv, Ukraine, February 2019

46. Adelaja, Sunday, History Makers Training: How to Plan, Structure and Achieve Your Life Goals for the Next 25 Years. Kyiv, Ukraine, February 2019

47. Adelaja, Sunday, System Building: The Key to Resolving Every Problem and Attaining Every Goal, Golden Truth Publishing 2018, Pg 183

Order directly on
Amazon Book Store

Now Available at

www.laternabooks.ng

1611 Adeola Hopewell Street
Victoria Island, Lagos

sales@laternabooks.ng

08033014462, 08100234441